John Thomas Boyle

Poems of Fancy and Imagination

John Thomas Boyle
Poems of Fancy and Imagination
ISBN/EAN: 9783744717557
Printed in Europe, USA, Canada, Australia, Japan
Cover: Foto ©Thomas Meinert / pixelio.de

More available books at **www.hansebooks.com**

POEMS

OF

FANCY AND IMAGINATION.

BY
JOHN T. BOYLE.

PRESS OF J. B. LIPPINCOTT COMPANY,
PHILADELPHIA.
1888.

CONTENTS.

	PAGE
FAIRY-LAND	5
MY PALACE IN THE AIR	39
TO FLORA'S VOICE	49
THE WARNING	54
LEGEND OF THE CROWN	58
STORY OF THE FORGET-ME-NOT	69
BALLAD OF COLIN CLOVER	77
LOVE IN A PALACE	89
THE ENCHANTERS; OR, THE DANCE OF DEATH	103
ALLIEGUNDABAGO:	119
Episode No. 1. The Mastodon	126
Episode No. 2. Off Cape Cod	135
Episode No. 3. A dream he dreamed	142
SUICIDE.—A VISION	151

FAIRY-LAND.

I do not know, nor do I care,
When it was, or how, or where
I gained the heart of fairy-land:
All I know and all I care—
  As celestial memory
  Of a rosy revery
  With gladd'ning song returns to me—
Is to feel that I was there!
There to see its charming sights;
There to taste its sweet delights;
There to revel in its blisses;
There to feast me with its kisses;
There to air my fretted mind
In its healing, balmy wind;
And there to let my fancy play
In childhood's golden holiday.
Oh, 'twas ravishingly rare
All the wonder I saw there!
Cloudless skies and healthful air;
Flow'ry meads and leafy alleys;
Sunny slopes and verdant valleys;

FAIRY-LAND.

Mountains rich in endless stores
Of rarest gems and priceless ores;
Glitt'ring fountains, rainbow sprayed;
Gay parterres in bloom arrayed;
Odorous prairies all berivered;
Isle-filled lakelets breeze beshivered;
Babbling waterfalls and fells
Hid in consecrated dells;
Grottos scintillant with gems,—
Earthly stars of Bethlehems;
Caves of mystic mysteries
Which no vulgar eye e'er sees;
Balm-trees ever blossoming
In a summer-tempered spring;
Others, from whose boughs, distended,
Luscious tempting fruits suspended;
Blissful views of Arcady;
Glimpses of Utopia's sea;
Regal Fancy's broad demesne,
Ruled by dainty fairy queen;
Where blithe music, song, and dance
Filled the breezes with romance,
And dissolved each earthly care—
Cark and sorrow—into air.

When into the land I chanced,
  I was greeted by a Fay,

Gloriously countenanced,
   With an eye as bright as day,
Whose drapery of dazzling light
All bewildered my dazed sight,
Till her magic arts supplied
Dull earth's defects, when, spirit-eyed,
I each fairy-scene descried.

Then, with gracious courtesies,
   Through an atmosphere of balm,
Led she me by whispering trees
   To where an Oriental calm
Echoed with the harmonies
Of fair Nature's minstrelsies.
Soon we came unto a dell
   Nestled in a sunny vale,
Pranked with fern and pimpernel,
   Daffodil, and lilies pale,
And besprent with eglantines,
Roses red, and columbines,
Lovingly caressed and kissed
By primrose and by amethyst;
All entangled tenderly
With clinging vines, which slenderly
Crept from laurel-shaded plots
Of pansies and forget-me-nots,

And with coyish dalliance wound
Their slender tendrils them around.

There, in a sequestered spot
  Of transporting greenery,
Close beside a spangled grot
  Fringed with rarest scenery,
Near an agate-pebbled fountain
Gurgling from o'erhanging mountain,
By a sombre forest, hoary
With romance and magic story,
Where the tuneful warblers shed
Their rapturous ecstasies o'erhead,
And the insects' soothing croon
  Lulled the drowsy airs to sleep,
Or impelled, with tranceful rune,
  Zephyr in his bed to creep,
Saw I, turning suddenly
By gnarled trunk of giant tree,
Nebulous and visionary,
All the world of myth and fairy,—
  Elf and nymph, and sportive fay,
Gnome, and genius, all were there;
  Goblin, sprite, and kelpie gay,—
Born of water, earth, and air,—
A countless train, a motley throng,
Floating on the breath of song,

Or, with gleesome mimicries,
Sporting in the dusk of trees,
Like hashished thoughts in reveries;
Or, in mirthful jollities,
Dancing with bacchantic glee
Through the bowers of Revelry;
Or in fountains glittering
Fluttering with glossy wing;
Or in wild absurdities
Venting their frivolities;
Or by nest of cooing dove
Tasting of the sweets of love;
While, unconscious, others dreamed
  'Mid the poppies' gorgeous bloom,
Or like starry glories streamed
  From acacia's soft perfume.

Habited were some in light
Too intense for mortal sight;
The effulgence of the sun
Was darkness in comparison.
Robed were others in the gray
Tissues of the garish day;
Or sarcenet of heaven's blue,
Edged with rarest flowers' hue.
Some were draped in noontide's shimmer,
And the pallid morn-star's glimmer;

Or were daintily arrayed
In gossamer of dappled shade;
Or in mellow-tinted beams
Angel-worked with gold of dreams;
Or in rainbow's changeful hues,
   Sun-thread blazed in fiery splendor,
By the nimble-witted Muse,
   With conceits grotesque and tender
In transparentness of waves,
   Or the flash of ruby cluster;
Or imp-woven dusk of caves
   Glossed with polished metal's lustre,
Some were garbed; or, in whiteness
Of the diamond's regal brightness;
While, celestially serene,
Robed in incandescent sheen,
Others sparkled through the green.

By prodigious aerolite,
Lichen-bossed and vine bedight;
In the music of a rill,
Which, laughing, leaped from dozing hill,
And unto my eyes displayed
Foam-flaked eddies, gemmed cascade;
While my chaperon, in dream,
   'Neath a Dryad-haunted tree
     By Delphic cave of mystery

Drowsed on couch of shade and beam,
   Stretchéd I, luxuriously,
On the moss of fenneled green,
   And with sweet complacency
Let my soul enjoy the scene,
And absorb the dulcet sounds
Which ravished the ethereal bounds.
Soon, athrough my fainting frame
   Felt I opiate languors creep,
While a lulling murmur came
   And softly soothed me into sleep;
Then mischievous Puck appeared,
Tricksy-faced and motley-geared,
And infused into my eyes
The discernment of the wise,
Till the influences of sight
Grasped the shadows, 'solved the light,
And opened to my wondering mind
The mysteries of fairy-kind.

Then across my vision streamed
   Shining troops of antic fays,
Who amid the foliage gleamed
   Like coy sunbeams through the haze,
And, in tranceful reveries,
I watched their giddy jollities.

Some on cobweb swings were swinging
   In the shadows of the shade,
Or the bluebells' bells were ringing
   'Mid the silence of the glade:
Others, where kind Nature spread
Velvet mosses for the tread
Of elf-feet, with lustrous ropes
   Of spider's silk skipped merrily;
Or adown the scented slopes
   Phantoms chased right cheerily;
Or on vibrant grasses swayed,
Else with airy Atoms strayed
Where the Microzoa played;
Or seesawed on beams of sun
   Set athwart the quiv'ring sprays,
Or hid and hooped in elfish fun
   In the umbra of the haze.

Mounted on eccentric steeds
Or ray-wheeled velocipedes,
   Or sliding down a sunbeam bright,
Babbling tipplers, in carouse,
   Chased the fascicles of light
Through the labyrinth of boughs
   With exuberance of sprite;
Or, in buffoonery of play,

With Illusions sped away
Through the glitter of the day.
Others, in transparent boats
Urged by evanescent motes,
Floated after thistle-blooms
Or vagrant down from Phœnix plumes;
Else from drooping branches swung,
Pendulous, the leaves among;
Or, tiptoe, on topmost spray
Whirled their fairy forms away
Into the great gaseous sea
Of Invisibility.

To and fro a motley rout
Breath-blown bubbles kicked about,
Or, in improvised balloons
Of webbed sunshine, sought the moons
In quest of moonshine, which to feed
Unto brains of priestly Creed,
While a masquerading crew,
Hurtled one another through,
Or with dewdrops pygmies pelted
Till they into ether melted.
Some, with quaintest juggleries,
Oped the buds of flow'rs and trees
And filled the air with drolleries.

Flirting with the Naiads in rill
They took fantastic shapes at will,
And tickled queen Mab's royalty
To gleesome risibility.
Awhile, with rosy mirth serene,
They stole the song from Music's queen
And wedded it to human voice,
Which filled the world with sweet rejoice.

Some were madly rollicking
   With the spectres of the bogs,
Else with toads were frolicking,
   Or at leapfrog with the frogs:
Others, where voluptuous Earth
   Bared her bosom to the sun,
Lullabied a croon of mirth,
   Till, impelled by imp of fun,
They scattered, with hilarious cries,
The swarming bees and butterflies.

There, in harlequin array,
Elf and ouphe in chatbird play,
Scared timid mote from sunny ray;
Teased songbirds till their drowsy notes
Fell tuneless from enangered throats;
Chased Echo's echo with rude mock
Till it died in scar of rock;

Then, with briberies, they won
The jocund chemist of the sun
To help them deck grass, shrub, and tree
With flow'rs and fruited oddity.

Some in jasmine hammocks swung
The budding lemon-trees among;
Where, lulled to sleep by locusts' rhe-r-r,
Or the drone of grasshopper,
They dreamed the dreams of childhood, and
Saw visions of the spirit-land.
Some in leafy wildernesses,
'Mid the drooping ferns and cresses,
Wooed coquettish Zephyrs till
Of them they'd their own sweet will;
Or with animated leaf
 'Mongst the slumb'rous foliage hid,
Listened to the garrulous grief
 Of complaining Katydid.

Sconced in hermit solitudes,
Where, halcyon-like, sweet Silence broods,
Nor sound of axe or gun intrudes,
Disturbed alone by whu-r-r and thrum
Of the pheasant's throbbing drum;

Or the nervous cleck-cleck-cleck
Of the red-head woodpeck's peck,
Or the liquid spink! spink! spink!
Of the turncoat bobolink;
Or the clear, keen, mellow gush
Of the music-throated thrush,—
Chosen ones 'mid rose and thyme
Set for men sweet thoughts for rhyme;
Or, with crucible and torch,
  Over Nature's prostrate form,
Strove within the noise and scorch
  Of an intellectual storm,
Till, with feverish unrest,
They wrung the secrets from her breast,
And allied them to the mind
Of the chosen of mankind:
Others, with felicity,
Uncaged the soul of Melody,
And fitted madrigals and glees
To Music's sylvan harmonies.
Some where hyacinthine gales
Fragranced soporific vales,
With gay birds of plumage rare
Thrilled with song the dreamless air,
Till the Sylphides of the breeze,
Enamoured, swooned in ecstasies,
And died in voiceless shrubberies.

Here and there marauding Sprites,
Esquired by malicious Frights,
On air barbs or fiery steeds,
Which Imagination breeds,
Armed with mimic swords of hate
From the armory of Fate,
Or gnome-fashioned sunshaft lances
Tipped with sting of Harpy glances,
Waged fierce war with fly and gnat,
Mosquitoes vile, and caverned bat,
Or ophidians of mire,
Else with scorpions of fire,
While, with savage bows and arrows,
  Shaped from the elastic air,
Others fought pugnacious sparrows
  Or grim spider in his lair.
Some the vagrant wasps attacked
Or the hornet castles racked,
While, exultant, others sacked
The ant-hills, or, with revelries,
Filched the treasured industries
Of the amber-cloistered bees.

As I gazed came to my ear,
  By the breath of Zephyrs borne,
Musically sweet and clear
  Mellow mot of Fairy horn;

Then, all faintly, as in dream,
  From the greenwood's rocky bounds,
Falcons' shriek and herons' scream,
  And the bay of Fairy hounds.
Then I heard, like imps of rain
  When they patter on the leaves
Or upon the flowered plain,
  Fairy footfalls, as from sheaves
Of the forest-garnered light.
  There emerged, all woodland geared,
And addressed my wond'ring sight,
  Elfin hunters, bowed and speared,
In pursuit of doe as white
  As the fleecy mists of June
When they glitter in the bright
  Noontide of the full-orbed moon.
Swift as flit the nimble airs
  When they dimple clovered grass,
Chasing myths of phantom Cares,
  Did the hunt and hunters pass,
And in the umbrageous green
Dissolved like spray from sun-kissed scene.

Then I saw, where warblers plumed
  Airily their dewy pinions
And the pink and fuchsia bloomed
  In the Tam'rand king's dominions,

Dilettante sipping dew
   From the golden buttercups,
While a philosophic few
   Mellowed all their hearts with sups
Of divinest nectar from
   The virgin lily's silver chalice,
Ray-distilled from precious gum
   By the wizard Amaryllis,
Or the prisoned waters which
The Magi thrall in crystal wall
   Of the Atom's diamond palace.

Crowned with halvéd amaranth
   Bacchanals by lotus tables
Couched on cushionings of Cynth,
   While they uttered witful fables;
And, in language quaint and sweet
   As the throb of Fancy's chime,
Gossiped with the passing fleet
   Eidolons of tireless Time,
Or discoursed of human kind
In words aerially refined,
Exploring every nook of mind;
Or listened to the fairy lore
Of sages of the days of yore,
While following celestial shadow
Through Utopia's Eldorado,

And from dishes silver white,
Or gravéd plates of golden light,
Banqueted, like Sybarite,
Off marmalades of lusciousness,
Locust thighs, with mint and cress,
Humbirds' brains, and tongues of quails,
And the spiced delights of snails,
Sauced with the deliciousness
  Of may-apples, haws, and cherries,
And the appetizing press
  Of the excellence of berries;
Or of ambered insects ta'en
By swart Mermen from the main;
Or the properties of grain
Steeped in saccharine of cane;
Or rare essences of meats
Dressed with the ambrosial sweets
Of jellied tamarinds and dates
From trees which bloom by Eden's gates
Candied citrons, figs, and grapes
From Avalon's enchanted capes;
Luscious pulp of mangosteen,
Flavors of vanilla bean;
Syllabubs of cocoa cream,
Whipt by Houries—in a dream—
To an evanescent foam,
Dulceted with mell of comb,

Tinctured with the breath of spice
And cinnamons of Paradise.
Some the toothsomeness of nuts
Tasted, with the daintiest cuts
Of pineapples and bananas
From Floridian savannas;
Or the hearts of melons iced
   With frosted air, and sunny peaches
Pregnant with delight and spiced
   By the gales of Persian reaches;
Or the ravishing express
Of pomegranate's lusciousness;
Or red-pulped oranges, which glow
In golden beauty by the flow
Of laughing waters, in the shade
By stately palm and olive made
In Vallombrosa's classic glade,
Where rare blooms and teeming vines
Enchant the spirit's Apennines,
And each dreaming sense enthralls
In Fantasy's cerulean halls.

Some on pink-fringed toadstools sat,
While they charged the air with chat;
Or, with nectared gossipings,
Gave delicious utterings
To undreamed thoughts of unthought things;

While from opalescent white
Goblets, of translucent light,
Or air-bubbles, cut in twain
By keen instruments of Spain,
Supped they liquors exquisite,
Twanged with spice of Attic wit;
Elixirs, which fruit-fays draugh
For the fairy-tribes to quaff,
Of the apricot and pear,
Nectarines and peaches rare,
Apples, quinces, gage, and plum,
Vinted by some fairy Mumm;
With bouquet from off the grapes
Which purple the Aonian capes;
Or in amber clusters shine
Athrough the em'rald-foliaged vine,
Where gay birds-of-paradise,
From the glare of Orient skies,
Shadow with their jewelled wings
Waters of Pierian springs;
Or which ripen in the breeze
Which fan th' effulgent deities
Of the happy isle-gemmed seas
Which skirt the soul's Hesperides.

In a rhododendroned dell,
Where the gray-green mosses fell

From gnarled branches in festoons,
   Like the hazy fringes set
   To Night's trailing folds of jet
By the planet-circling moons;
In the pine-trees' shadows, where
   The timid sunbeams, frightened, quivered,
And the spirits of the air
   'Mid the foliage sat and shivered;
Where the subtle-gliding snake
Chased the squirrel through the brake,
Or, with fascinations dire,
Lured rash birds to coil of ire;
Where, through fear, the lizard slid
   Like a flash in cleft of rock,
And the saucy catbird chid
   Silence with his scornful mock;
There, where sleek-furred mole and mouse
Wassailed in the muskrat's house,
Or the black-coat beetle rolled
His egg-stored balls; where rabbits holed,
And the mottled gem-brained toad
Leaped along the deer-lick road;
Where tortoise hid, and truant snail
Slimed the ant's erratic trail;
Where the chatt'ring jaybird prated
And the cooing ring-dove mated,
Saw I, with discerning eyes,

In the freckle spots of shade,
  Gaudy-tricked and sheen-arrayed,
Fairy lovers, heard their sighs,
As, by brookside, 'mid the fern,
  Arm in arm they, loitering, walked;
Or aside the prattling burn
  With the misty Naiads talked;
Or where grasses, vine-entangled,
Were with dandelions bespangled;
There where Summer, proud as bride
  When she from the altar goes,
Treads on roses in her pride,
  While her fond eye overflows
With joy-drops, which, by sylvan bowers,
Fall and gender fragrant flowers;
Or where dimpling waters pooled
And the trout and minnow schooled;
Where beetle-shrub and spider sped
O'er flaccid waters, while o'erhead
All the white-faced elders braided
With the hazel leaves, and shaded
Card'nal-flowered, blue-flagged edges
Of the fuzzy, foxtailed sedges;
Where gay gladiolas rimmed
The glassy meres all swallow-skimmed,
While the elfin boatmen swayed
  In their lily-leaf canoes

And the air-born children played
  'Mongst the rushes of the ooze,
Saw I them environed by
  Genii guardians of the spot,
  Or denizens of haunted grot,
Sit luxurious and eye
Each the other,—Oh, how shy!
Scarcely speaking with their lips,
Only with their finger-tips;
Or that mystic language which
  Love expresses feelings by,
Timid glances, nervous twitch,
  Tell-tale blush, and philtered sigh;
Or 'neath spice-wood sassafrases
  By the wild witch-hazel tree,
Sheltered by the pompous grasses,
  Robed in vestal purity,
Saw I them, with cheeks afire,
Wantoning with sweet desire;
While their lips beguiled with words
Tenderer than notes of birds,
Enrapturing the breathless gales
With love-songs and am'rous tales,
Till in gondolas of gleams,
They floated down celestial streams
Into the summer sea of dreams.

Others saw I through the gloom
  Of a fountain's silvered mist,
  Where blushed Iris, Phœbus-kissed,
Nestling where magnolias' bloom
Drowned the breezes in perfume;
Or where oleanders scent
With geranium odors blent,
Stretched on beds of mignonettes
Or swards of virgin violets;
In an atmosphere of sighs
Laden with the balm of skies.
Raptured in a chaste embrace,
Cheek to cheek or face to face,
Fondly dreaming, naught expressing,
Each the other's heart addressing
In the language of caress,
Dalliance, and amorous press,
Wishing, secretly, the while,
  Wishes which they dare not utter,—
Dainty wishes, tinged with guile,
  Such as set young hearts aflutter,
While their spirits, in the skies
Of the lover's Paradise,
Revelled in the wine of bliss
Pressed by love from fruity kiss.

Like elect of the sublime,
Never making note of time,
'Tranced, and all absorbed, I lay
Till the purple of the day
Melted into twilight's gray,
And the harbinger of night
Twinkled on my chrismed sight,
While the spell of Silence fell,
O'er lake, mountain, mead, and dell,
And the fitful shadows shed
Their holy influences and spread
O'er earth a superstitious dread.
Then beside the vagaries
Of the mock-bird's ecstasies
And the plover's aqueous cry
And the wild swan's vesper sigh
And the doleful, wailing, shrill
Note of circling whippoorwill
And the screech-owl's dismal "hoot,"
Mingled with the nighthawk's "scoot,"
And from crevices of rocks
The sly bark of wily fox,
Wedded to the cry of loon,
  Shriek of bittern, "caw" of crow,
With the marsh-frog's croaking croon
  And the low of fawn and doe,

Fell athrough the atmosphere
All acutely on my ear.
Th' enrapturing harmonies
Of the wind-harp's symphonies,
And the notes of Ariel's flute,
  Trill of pipe, and sigh of reed,
Dainty twang of elfin lute,
  With the voice of wood and mead;
And I heard the mellow gush
Of the forest's solemn hush;
Heard the waves of darkness flowing,
Soughing, sighing, coming, going,
And the lowly glowworms glowing;
From the dusky hills of dreams
Heard the flow of silent streams;
Heard the bells of Fancy ringing;
Heard the tender grasses springing;
Heard the tired convolvuluses
  Close their fragile leaves to sleep,
And the airs, with childish fusses,
  Into cave and flower creep;
Heard the flutter of Ouphe wing;
Heard the Dryads' gossiping;
Heard the starry splendor, falling
  On the mist, like flake on wave,
And the darkling shadows calling
  Phantoms from each bat-filled cave;

From the bounds of distance heard
The fantasies of Cynthia's bird;
And, blending with the sweet rejoice
Of dear Nature's soothing voice,
Heard the warbling spirits and
The bugle notes of Fairy-land.

Soon, from out the pearly haze
  Of the moonlit atmosphere,
Sudden as a meteor's blaze,
  Came a fairy pioneer;
And, above the glist'ning mead,
Floated on his firefly steed,
Till where spread a dainty plot
Of lum'nous mosses, by a grot
Of melancholy mysteries,
'Neath the boughs of fragrant trees,
Stopped, and fingering magic key,
Blew bugle-notes of melody,
Which, as flowers' subtle scent
Fills the space of firmament,
Penetrated each recess
Of rock and brambled wilderness,
And bade each dreamy elf and fay
To robe and thread the jovial way
Which led to sport and revelry,
And mirth and fairy jubilee.

Then bourgeoned from bud and flower,
Tuft and plume and odorous bower,
Like the regal exhalations
  Of the opium-fevered mind,
All the whimsical creations
  Of terrestrial fairy-kind;
And, on wingéd footsteps, flew
T'ward the chosen rendezvous.
Will-o'-wisp his wizard light,
Lit and showed them through the night,
And his frisky brother Jack-
O'-th'-lantern spooked the track,
And, lowering his pallid fire,
Led them safe past bog and mire,
Till, with antique flame-wood lamp,
Goblin, from his cedrine camp
O'er rock, stream, and briery way,
Led them by the haunted way.

All assembled, joyously,
  I' th' glimpses o' th' moon,
    To the music of the air
Fell their feet as noiselessly
  As petals fall from crown of June,
    Or as shade on noontide's glare;
Or as imaged shapes that dance
In a tender maiden's glance;

In the waltz's am'rous whirl
Or fandango's tinkling twirl,
Else on polka's giddy wing
Round and round enchanted ring.

From his vigil in Oaktower
Woodtick ticked the midnight hour,
And the death-watch by the bed
Of ill mortal drooped his head;
While the vampire and the ghoul,
To the "hoot" of mousing owl,
Flapped their fiendish wings and flew
To cypress shade and mournful yew.

High in heav'n the loving moon,
   Like a vestal, robed in white,
Floating in eternal noon,
   Glorified the dusky night,
And glossed, with rare effulgency,
The sleeping earth and slumb'rous sea.

Amor, musing in the shade
Of the voiceless everglade,
Held in thrall by magic spell
Of enchantress Philomel,
Sighed love-pæans in her praise,
Wooing Dian's ardent gaze

Till he won it; when, as wave
   Captures star with crystal hand
And holds it prisoner in cave
   Of subaqueous wonderland,
So he caught her in embrace,
Kissed the blushes from her face,
Until, ravished with delight,
He fainted in the arms of Night.

Then stole gently to my ears
Seraph notes of crystal spheres,
And from off the breeze's wing
Sweet airs of fairy trumpeting.
Faintly, quaintly, swelling nearer,
   Like the pine's Æolian sighing,
Drew the echoes, sweeter, clearer,
   Till they on my ears fell dying;
While upon their wingéd steeds,
Which the wind of Cloudland breeds,
Appeared the trumpeters, and then,
Like glint, from gloom of bosky glen,
With ray swords and starbeam spears,
A troop of elfin cavaliers.
Following 'neath banners white,
With austral blazonings bedight
And streamers of celestial light,
From defile and sultry shade,

Panoplied in sheen of steel,
Which the master gnomes anneal,
Came a knightly cavalcade,
Encircling a gemmed array
Of elfin loveliness, so bright
That Jealousy and envious Night,
Writhing, drew themselves away
In exuberance of pain
Which tortured them to thoughts insane,
And poured on sympathizing air
The agonies of their despair.
As king-stone of diadems
  Glistens with transcendent lustre
'Mid the radiance of gems
  Which adorn the dazzling cluster,
So, amid the galaxy
  Of beauty so refined and airy,
Shone, in peerless majesty,
  Mab, the virgin queen of fairy.

Imagination ne'er allured
  From the Eden of the mind,
Never Fancy miniatured
  To the eye of artist-kind,
Vision so supremely fair
As this creature of the air;
Ne'er can words to mind convey

The glory of her bright array;
Nor rapt pencil e'er express
The fulness of her loveliness;
Nor cunning chisel hope to trace
Her excellence of form and face:
In her person were combined
All the graces of her kind;
Perfect was she as a star,
Naught to censure, naught to mar.

Col'optera and lantern-fly
From their weary watch on high
Did her radiance descry,
And signalled to elf sentinel,
Who vigil kept at holy well,
And he, through golden trumpet-flow'r,
To master of the festive hour.
Instant, as when sunclouds shake
From drowsy wings on rippling lake
The down of calm, and all is still:
Attracted by his magnet will,
At his imperial command,
Expressed by wave of magic wand,
The dancing ceased. *Ad interim,*
As in vast cathedrals dim
   Rapt souls, on wings of melody,

Upborne on airs of chaunt and hymn,
Attain the heights of ecstasy;
  And there through myrrhy incense skim
O'er agitated waves of air,
  And then, with pinions, love-enchained,
Sink to hush of silent prayer;
So fell, like spell of organed psalm,
Upon the scene a holy calm,
  And Silence for a moment reigned.

Then, from heart of tranquil dell,
Floated, with melodious swell,
A mockingbird's ethereal joy;
Subdued at first, and maiden coy,
Then rising, swelling nigh and nigher,
Warbling, with gay coquetries,
His répertoire of woodland glees,
Laughing, twitt'ring, piping, sighing,
Chirping, whistling, oooing, crying,
Climbing, soaring high and higher,
Till, with airs of spirit choir,
Its own notes blent so gloriously
That a passing seraph stopped
  A blissful moment in career,
And from bounds of distance dropped
  The matchless melody to hear.

Then sliding from celestial heights
Of harmonious delights,
Through clewless labyrinths of sound,
Its notes flew in and out and round
In delirious ecstasies
Of derisive melodies,
Which, with 'wakened catbird's jangle,
Caught fair Nature's self in tangle,
And the voices of the night
'Woke to transports of delight,
Until, melted into glee,
  The aspened shade and dewy green
Chimed with chorused jubilee
  Of fairies' welcome to their queen.

Then enveloped all the scene
Lucid mists of dazzling sheen,
And blue vapors, all aglow
With the colors of the bow,
Which expressed in bold relief
Each vinéd rock and blade and leaf
And portrayed, with sunlight power,
Sprite and fay and elfin flower.
Puck I saw, and Ariel,
Oberon, and Fariel,
Atom, Pin, and Midge, and Buzz,
Pink, and Pea, Pip, Myth, and Fuzz;

And each other elf and fay
Which joyed our childhood's holiday
And ever with our fancies play.
Heavenly music from the plain
Filled the tissues of my brain,
Charged the airs with nonchalance,
And, beneath the queenly glance,
Buoyed the fairies in their dance.

Then, athrough the foliage, I
   Saw, against the sombre air,
Forms fantastic, giant high,
   With great eyes of astral glare,
Who, with smile or weird grimace
Playing o'er each changeful face,
Gazed upon the scene, until
Shadow, winging from the hill,
Enfolded them in mist of streams
Which shimmer through the vale of dreams.
Then I saw, from secret nook,
Peering goblins, wraith, and spook;
And from cone-tipped evergreens,
   Where clung vine and mistletoe,
Nymphs peeking coyly from leaf-screens,
   Or shad'wy flitting to and fro.
Then athrough the atmosphere

Floated vaguely, soft and clear,
The herald notes of Chanticleer;
And, in flash of dawning day,
The blissful vision paled away.

MY PALACE IN THE AIR.

A PEERLESS palace, divinely fair,
Have I fashioned, with matchless care,
Off in the amethystine air.

Ethereally, its walls uprear
Into the lucid atmosphere,
Pale as a star when day draws near.

Its azure roofs transcend in height
Till, fading in the infinite,
They mock the keenest grasp of sight.

Turret, tower, and minaret,
Wrought out of midnight's sheen and jet,
On its shadowy walls are set.

Its spires and towers of radiant stone,
Hewn from the sun's enchanted zone,
Ambitious, seek the Air-King's throne.

Scintillant spans of golden light
Uphold its ceilings of sky, alight
With twinkling stars exceeding bright.

MY PALACE IN THE AIR.

Its columns of crystalled hyacinth,
With dreamy capitals of Corinth,
Are sheened from astragal to plinth.

Of topazed rays are its balustrades,
Solid moonbeams its colonnades,
Marbled snow-flakes its promenades.

Each of its adamantine floors
Is tessellated with polished ores
Studded with rubies and Kohinoors.

Yet does it seem as if it were
Builded out of naught but air,
So very dream-like 'tis and fair.

Its spacious chambers, with matchless care,
Are hung with laces of frosted air
And furnished artfully, debonair!

Its diamond panes, celestially,
Sparkle in far-off majesty
Like the sun-kissed waves of a summer sea.

All earthly halls its hall outvies,
Ceiled with kaleidoscopic skies,
Aurora-tinged with gorgeous dyes.

From off its circling walls of blue
A dome, cyclopean, clear as dew,
Studded with brilliants of every hue,

Swells into space, and glints in light,
Compared with which noon's glare is night,
Blinding the unaccustomed sight.

'Neath its arches, through endless day
Fountains of living waters play,
Cooling the airs with fragrant spray.

Its tapestries of limpid blues,
Glorified with dissolving views,
Broidered with rainbow's wealth of hues,

Are limned with tracery of gems,
Sceptres ar'besqued with diadems,
Emerald leaves with garnet stems

Flecked with lustrous filigrees,
With roses, and anemones,
Winged butterflies, and birds, and bees.

'Tis carpeted with velveteen
Of fairy mosses and evergreen,
Bossed with flowers and dewdrops' sheen.

MY PALACE IN THE AIR.

Winding stairs of light and shade,
With genii-fashioned balustrade
All sheen of radiance inlaid,

Lead to celestial galleries,
Such as rapt dreamer, dreaming, sees
When solving heavenly mysteries.

There pictures by Fancy's pencil draught,
Schemes from the busy brain of Thought,
Statues Imagination wrought,

Enchant the sight and fill the mind
With glorious deeds, of human kind,
In nichéd walls, or stand combined

With cabinets of Art's device,
Which Luxury's self might all suffice,
Of airy turquois clear as ice,

Filled with exquisite treasures fair
Drawn from the ocean, earth, and air,—
Magnificent! beyond compare.

After the carkings of the day,
My spirit, spurning its home of clay,
Soars to my Palace far away.

Free as an eagle, unconfined
As the flight of the wayward wind,
It leaves my slothful clay behind,

And with it care and misery,
All which we helpless mortals see
Drifting to immortality;

And while men toil in anxious pain,
Bartering their souls for sordid gain,
Seeking that which they seek in vain,

I in my palace, all alone,
With brooding Silence on a throne,
List'ning the air-waves' hollow moan,

Sit, like a holy evangelist
Beside the heavenly eucharist,
Quaffing from sangreal of amethyst

The mellow joy of a golden wine
Crushed from the heart of a grape divine
Grown in mine airy Palestine.

High o'er the sorrowing vale of tears
I watch the shades of departed years,
And list to the music of the spheres.

MY PALACE IN THE AIR.

Gazing where Saturn's crimson bars
Flash through the glittering of stars,
Flushed with the sanguine glow of Mars,

I seek that blissful realm which lies
Deep in the bosom of the skies,—
The soul-absorbing Paradise.

Fond but vainly I sit and peer,
With eyes which gleam like eyes of seer,
Into the radiant atmosphere,

Hoping by human faith to see
The elysium of Mystery,
Its stream of life and mystic tree,

Its pearly gates, its jewelled walls,
Its shining mansions and blissful halls,
O'er which God's glory forever falls,

Its streets of sheen, its marvellous throne
In the city's glitter, all alone,
Resting on kingdoms overthrown;

But, blinded by empyrean blaze,
Shrinking, in wonder and amaze,
Humbled, I turn my 'wildered gaze

And see, through the airy ocean's spray,
Ethereal islands, far away
'Mid the starry-crested waves of day,

Which seem like beryls set in a lake
Of molten brilliants, whose ripples break
'Gainst golden foreland in opal flake,—

Those blessed isles which the ancient wise
Deemed the terrestrial Paradise
Floating midway 'tween earth and skies,—

Cloudland, with its gorgeous sights,
Its airy splendors, its sweet delights,
Which, dreaming, we taste in summer nights,

Its sapphire-blazing peaks, which rear
From luminous vales, intensely clear,
Into the lucent atmosphere,

Hollowed with grottos all alight
With scintillant drops of stalactite
And driftings of splendrous stalagmite;

Floored with tufa of crystalled foam,
In the fashion of ancient Rome,
Cunningly veined by skilful gnome;

Its sparkling plumes, like feathers of snow,
Drifting which way the winds do blow,
With crags of silver flashing below;

Its slopes, with palaces and towers,
Pavilions weird with radiant bowers,
'Mid wilds of amaranthine flowers;

Its obelisks of pearl, half hid
By cenotaphs of saints, amid
Shadows of stately pyramid

Constructed each and every one
From lustrous blocks of chalcedon,
Quarried out of the noonday sun.

No earthly potentate, I opine,
Ever reared a palace like to mine,—
So grand, so noble, so divine!

Reclused, by shore of summer sea,
On cloud-cushioned couch of ivory,
Beneath a luscious-fruited tree,

Lulled to sleep by melodies
Swelling up from seas and trees
On amorous balm-laden breeze,

MY PALACE IN THE AIR.

I dream such dreams as never before
Mortal dreamed this side Death's door,
Soothed with poppy or hellebore:

Of heroes, gods, and godlike men,
Ghost, and shadow, and haunted glen,
Of fairy rose-bowered denizen;

Of horrid monsters, huge and grim;
Of genii, giant, and pygmy trim;
Of angel, seraph, and cherubim;

Of death and life so transitory,
Hell with its terrors, purgatory,
And heaven's pure and radiant glory—

And, oh! may the regality
Of my shadowy principality
Grow into heaven's reality!

What care I for silver or gold,
Fleeting honors, houses, or wold?
In my palace I've wealth untold,—

Gems of wisdom and treasures of mind
Out of the ages, doubly refined
By th' elected of mankind,

MY PALACE IN THE AIR.

Diamonds of Philosophy,
Gold from the drift of History,
Pearls from the sea of Poetry:

Need I more? I live in content
With that which kind heaven has lent
To cheer my spirit in banishment.

What though th' infatuated crowd
Scornfully slight and taunt aloud,
And mist my mind in sorrows cloud?

Yet, steeped in sweet philosophy,
I grieve for all their misery,
And pity those who pity me.

Thus, when my fainting spirit tires
Of the world and its vain desires,
Into my palace it retires,

And in the boundless realm of mind,
With kindred spirits always find
The happiness for me designed.

Ah me! From the dreamy far away
My spirit seeks its crypt of clay,
And my airy palace fades away.

TO FLORA'S VOICE.

Soul of music shrined in earth,
Offspring of celestial birth,
Thou that swayest mind and heart
Through divinity of Art,
To my consciousness impart
Thy secret,—who, and what thou art!
Ne'er, since mother's lullabies
Soothed my senses, closed my eyes,
Have I heard such melody
From the lips of minstrelsy;
Ne'er, from foliage or sea,
Such mellifluous harmony.

Plaint of ocean's murm'ring shell,
Sigh of zephyr, croon of dell,
In thy blissful warblings dwell;
Yea, all sweet sounds of earth and sea,
Absorbèd, lose themselves in thee—
Tell me, soul of music, tell,
Whence thou comest, where dost dwell?

TO FLORA'S VOICE.

Ne'er did note of feathered sprite
Yield me such intense delight;
Ne'er did murmur of a rill,
Carol of enchanted hill,
Charge with such voluptuous thrill
Or so captivate my will:
Never voice of mead or brook,
Chaunt of bard or song of book,
Nor Æolian symphony,
Seem so musical to me!

Wafted by thy sorceries,
My soul, afloat, skims airy seas,
Till, encompassed by the moon,
All deliriously I swoon,
As to brain, through ravished ear,
Steal thy notes to bless and cheer!—
Tell me, charmer, what thou be
That utterest such witchery?

Lilied strains of summer airs
Breathed by saints at evening prayers;
Inspirations wreathed and wound
With the roses of sweet sound,
Glorify thy carollings,
Fit thy notes to seraph wings,

TO FLORA'S VOICE.

And allure my soul to rise
From Earth's dross to bliss of skies.
Is it love inspires thy strain,
Dulcifies thy rapt refrain?
Is it love that fires my brain
As I listen? Thought divine!
I am thine, and thou art mine!

Say, enchanting mystery,
Art angelic ecstasy
'Scaped athrough the sheeny portals
Of the home of the immortals?
Or rapt joy by heaven sent
To cheer our souls in banishment?
Art thou Orpheus himself
Sporting as a wanton elf,
Or faint echo of his lyre
Mellowed with Promethean fire
For the use of earthly choir?
Or dying breath of cherubim?
Thou essence of terrestrial hymn!

We hear thee, yet we see thee not;
   We feel thy power, confess its sway,
As rising, like a bugle's mot,
   It melts into a golden lay

So aerial, soft and clear,
Cherubs stoop from heaven to hear,
While the envious songsters spring
From bright dreams on flutt'ring wing,
And imbibe from dulcet strain
The joy which is akin to pain,
Till their hearts in overflow
Flood the woods and fields below.

Born thou wert amongst the Fairies,
   Child of Harmony and Tune!
Nurtured by the blithe canaries
   In a never-ending June;
Thence thou 'scaped in sportive mirth,
And, gleeful, hid thee in a birth,
Whence thy spirit, ever going,
Welleth like a streamlet flowing,
Breaking on enraptured ears
   With a melody divine,
Giv'n thee by the tuneful spheres,
   To enchant, and to refine.

As elf winds adown the sea
Trip it with Euphrosyne
To an unheard symphony,
Thrilling, like the breath of fame,
The angel of my languid frame,

Dost thou come; and as thy notes
Flood my soul as sunshine floats,
  Dreaming, I faint;
  And, like a saint,
  Bewinged I rise
  Unto the skies,
And list to the airs of Paradise.

THE WARNING.

Dainty maid with queenly tread,
Sunny hair all ringlettéd,
Eyes like those of the gazelle,
Forehead smooth as pearl of shell,—
　　Beware!
He'll betray! oh, he'll betray!
　　Away! away!
Listen what the Sibyls say:
"His promises are debonair,
His winning smiles beyond compare,
His honeyed words as light as air,—
　　Forbear!
Ere he mesh thee in his snare,
Ere he fills thy mind with care,
　　Pray, oh, pray!
Lest, when demons rule the hour,
And thou dreamest in Love's bower,
He will filch from thee thy dower,
　　And away
With the sunshine of thy day,
With the song which cheers thy way,

And the gem which glows serene
In thy bosom, beauty's queen!"

As the skies of Samarcand,
By electric sparkles fanned,
Are his eyes,—their satyred fires
Fuelled with his fierce desires.
In them lurketh Astrophel,
Forging mimic shafts of hell,
Which he tips with subtle glances,
Cruel as the steel of lances,
Which, through maidens' hearts that languish
In a dreamy love-lorn anguish,
Shooteth he, until they die
The death of deaths with frantic sigh.
Guard thy breast with triple plate
Now, before it be too late!
Fly them, else in mire of shame
Like-snow flake smirched will melt thy fame.

On his lips, bedewed with roses,
Where a siren's smile reposes,
Lurks a spell whose fragrant breath
Wooes thee to a living death;
In their ecstasy of kisses,
Which to thee seem angel blisses,

Coils an asp, whose cruelty
Bears destruction unto thee!
Then, maiden of the golden hair,
And haloed brow unmarked with care,
　　　Beware!
Lest, moaning, thou wilt sit and sing,
Thy tears downfalling on his ring,
" Ah, well-a-day! ah, well-a-day!
He only kissed me to betray!"

Round the taper of his fingers
Spells of an enchanter lingers,
And they permeate thy frame
With the subtleness of flame,
Till thy senses, sleeping, lie
Underneath a poppied sigh,
And thine immortality
Under seas of misery.
When he clasps thy tiny hand,
Fly thy thoughts to fairy-land;
When the spark of fell desire
Flashes to consuming fire,
Fly before that tragic thrill
Leaves thy body pale and chill!

Oh! his princely words are sweet
As he kneeleth at thy feet,

Suing thee, and wooing thee,
As if thou wert a mystery
Shrined within humanity;
While the glamour of his guile,
Lurking in insidious smile,
Allures thy spirit, craftily,
Into the glooms of infamy.
As to thirsty flower the dew,
Are his gracious words to you;
    Yet, beware!
    Take care!
For the mystic, Amorat,
In his wisdom, sayeth that
"Many a maiden's heart is wrung
Through the wiles of glozing tongue."
    Take care! take care!
    Beware! beware!

LEGEND OF THE CROWN.

    Enthroned in regal state,
    With sable-ermined robe
Of Tyrian purple, and breastplate
    Of laminated gold,
    Glittering with wealth untold;
Hand grasping gold-traced iron sceptre,
Tipped with argent ring-winged node,
Beneath gem-eyed ebony raven
Perched on an enambered globe;
    O'ershadowed by Death's wing,
    , All gloomily,
By beetling crag of maelstromed sea
    Sat Norland's sapient king.

    His seer-like beard
    So weird appeared
That base-born churls gazed, dazed, and feared;
    While his thin hair,
      Blanched white as snow
      Through royal woe,
    Flowed dreamily upon the air.

Anear him sat enthroned,
Like rosy nymph 'mongst lily-featured naiads,
Amid the splendor of attendant maids,
   In peerless beauty, like
      The full-orbed moon enzoned
     By galaxy of stars,
'Mid glint of battle-axe and pike,
Upborne by bronze-helmed sons of Mars,
    Seraphically fair,
Malvina his soul's pride,
Loved more than world beside,
   His only child and heir.

   By royal summons of command,
About him, ranged on either hand,
A belted, mail-clad band,
   His feuds and courtiers stand.

Then, from his head, his crown,
   Superlatively grand,
He raised, with kingly frown,
   And held in his right hand.

   From its gemmed circles streamed,
  And ravishingly gleamed,

A beamy light
So dazzling pure,
That scarce the unaccustomed sight
Its brilliance could endure.

"This,"—while he sighed,
He cried,—
"With mine own star-eyed
Malvina as a bride,
As Odin reigneth, and I live,
Will I give
To him
Who, stout of heart and strong of limb,
Braves yon seething waves,
And from the fury of the sea
Returns it all unharmed to me."

Out in the 'strom,
Amid the foam,
The guerdon fell.
Then, from coral cell,
And spangled caves,
The elves of waves
Upreared,
With faces ghast and seared,
And through the clear
Bright atmosphere

Of spectre-crested sea,
>Exultantly,
And with a maddening wild delight,
Snatched it with eager hands from sight.

Fair as the harbinger of day,
Sweet as the apple-bloom of May,
>All queen-arrayed,
But pale as the wan face of death—
Scarce caught the nimble airs her breath—
>Awaited the expectant maid.

With timid glances, half afraid,
Gazed she on her suitors grand,
>As they stood,
>In eager mood,
>All desiring,
>And aspiring,
To the fortune of her hand.

Within her throbbing breast of care,
Love fluttered like a dove in snare;
And to her sorrowing self she sighed,
As one gazed on her tender-eyed,
>"Oh that he,
>Through love of me,
Would brave the fierceness of the sea!—
O God of gods, be kind to him and kind to me!"

Far and wide,
Up the shore,
With deeper roar,
Chased by fierce breakers surged the tide.

Dashing, crashing,
With rude shocks,
'Gainst the storm-defying rocks,
Seething, hissing,
Now cloud-kissing,
Then deep under,
Burst the wind-hurled waves asunder,
Quivering earth like bolts of thunder.

Fearfully the faint-heart brood
Above the raging ocean stood.

The dreadful terrors of the flood
Dissolved their courage, chilled their blood.

Before their ruler stood confessed
The secret of each craven breast.

Then, with self-conscious bearing proud,
From the deep silence of the crowd
Stepped dauntless Rolla of the main,
Whose castle glowed in clouds of Spain;

Son of banished Eric, who,
   With his steel-ribbed ships of might,
Sailed conqueringly the South Seas through,
   Despoiling shores with ruthless blight.

With a pleasurable pain,
   Offspring of a sweet delight,
Gazed the maiden on the main
   Through sad tears which dimmed her sight.
Then, while her swelling breast heaved full with sighs,
Her soul glanced love into his longing eyes,
While breathed he silent prayer unto the skies,
"O Odin, god of gods! give ear. to me,
And shape to joy my future destiny!"

With stately mien and courtly tread
   Advanced he to the regal seat,
Full low he bowed his noble head
   To gain the monarch's kindly greet:
Awhile the heralds with acclaim
Declared his lineage and his name,
And north and south and east and west,
Proclaimed the purpose of the kingly breast.

    Before the maid,
      Stayed by his blade,
  He kneeled. All tremblingly,
      First her hand,

Then his brand,
Kissèd he,
While he whispered, "Without thee,
What were all this world to me?"

Conscious love, like red sunrise
When it tints the seas and skies,
Rosed her cheeks and lit her eyes:
Wild heaved her breast with smothered sighs.

In a tranceful ecstasy
From her fascination, he
Turned towards the angry sea.

Where towered battlements upreared,
There Scald and Berserks gaunt,
With Sagaman sat, while Harpers hoar
Upraised the hymn and chaunt.

From ivied tower and gnarlèd oak
Hoarse was heard the raven's croak.

Where the shimmering waters sprayed,
Where the glittering sunlight beamed,
Sportively the dolphins played,
Shrill the cruel cormorant screamed.

Shuddered Life and fluttered Death,
Pitying Nature held her breath,

As in the yawning jaws of ocean,
  From beetling crag beneath the tower,
They saw him plunge with quivering motion,
  Beheld the greedy waves devour.

  As when angered lightnings fall,
  Or sudden dangers men appall,
  Breathless stood they, one and all.

  Like a saint in stone, the maiden,
  All her soul with anguish laden,
  With her thoughts engulfed in sea,
  Sat and gazed all prayerfully;

  And the dying king, with shudder,
  Like a galley 'reft of rudder,
  Swayed and groaned with every motion
  Of the whirlpooled fiends of ocean.

  Dread silence reigned, while waxed intense
  The horrid torture of suspense!

  "Huzza! huzza! huzza!"
  Mingles with the passing flaw.
      "See! see!
      'Tis he, 'tis he!"

See, his doughty arm uprears!
    Lo! behold
    The crown of gold!
Above the waves his face appears.

In the dizzy circling swirl
Of the maelstrom's seething whirl,
'Mid its fierce convulsive throes,
Round and round and round he goes.

Celestial Hope and pallid Fear
Gaze through the fainting atmosphere;
With fervent words and pleading breath
They intercede for him with Death.

At her dragon-guarded gates,
Grim and lowering, Hela waits!
Beside her weave the dark-browed Fates.

    Crooning dirges,
    Sob the surges.

Love, from her ethereal steeps,
Looks through clouded eyes and weeps.

    Pity sighs;
    Envy dies.

Through the palpitating airs
Speed Rolla's and the maiden's prayers.

Throned amid revolving spheres
  With Frigga by his side,
Majestic Odin sits and hears,
  And scans the treacherous tide.

Obedient to his sovereign will,
  His raven, Huguin, flies
Swifter than light, through ether's chill,
  To cloud-land's dreamy skies;
And, at his bid, like thunderbolt,
  His sun-eyed eagle falls
Where maddened whirlpool, in revolt,
  Bold Rolla's limbs enthralls.
Its talons grasp his floating curls,
  The hand-held crown its beak,
While from the hellward whirlpool whirls,
  And from the ghastly reek,—
Awhile the baffled monster clings,
  And round his form his briny arms
And subtlest glamours deftly flings,
  With all his salamandrine charms,—
Buoys him with its powerful wings
Athrough the breakers' sullen roar,
Until he stands on Safety's shore.

Rave the disappointed waves,
  As they sunder,
  Growling thunder,
From their monster-haunted caves.
Screams, as shrieks the thwarted sea,
Odin's bird triumphantly.
Sunbeams splendor all its form;
 Till, like a phœnix-wingéd fire,
 Mounting high, and mounting higher!
It passes to the realm of storm;
Where, in a cloud as red as slaughter,
It vanished like foam-flake in water.

Then from the skies' effulgency
Came voice of rarest melody,
Which fell upon each listening ear
In tones which rung celestial clear:
  "Ne'er despair!
 For the true hearts are the fair,
 And brave spirits kingdoms are;
  Through willing ears
  Great Odin hears,
And hearing, grants as virtue's meed
Success to every noble deed
  When urged by guileless prayer."

STORY OF THE FORGET-ME-NOT.

Earth shrinking from the ardent gaze of Day,
Diana's tender smile was fondly waiting,
When, in the sombre shadow of a wood
Which fringed the margin of an Alpine lake,
A Knight and Lady wooed the fickle breeze.
Bright were her eyes; beyond compare her form,
So like a Sylph's that o'er the mead she moved
Scarce bending grass-blades 'neath her airy tread.
Her cheeks and lips were hued so delicate
That roses, gazing, blushed a deeper red;
While envious lilies drooped their pallid heads
And filled the amorous airs with fragrant sighs.
Graced was the Knight with all Apollo's charms
Such as no maiden, seeing, could resist;
Or, if she did, her fluttering heart would bear
Forever traces of the love-plumed shaft.
Arm twined in arm, with fond reliance filled,
Like confidence upon the arm of might
She strayed, and gazing in his gracious eyes,
Thrilled all his bosom with electric words
Which moved him to an ecstasy of bliss.

Before them, like a shimmering glory, lay
The placid waters of the sylvan lake;
And on its bosom, like an emerald mount
Dissolving in a sea of molten gems
Embossed with smiling clumps of od'rous flowers,
An island slumbered in a golden trance.
With longing eyes she gazed upon its banks,
And sighed a maiden's wish that she might wear
A flower from its Summer-painted strand.
Her every wish his law, her smile his heaven,
He left her side; and, instant, from the bank
Plunged headlong in the crystal tide and clove
With love-nerved arm the chill, elastic flood,
And breathless landed on the distant beach.
With dainty touch he culled the fragrant mead,
And with bouquet of azure-tinted flowers,
Like brave Leander strove to reach his love.,

With jealous eyes the foam-engendered Naiads,
Urged by the ferine demon of the depths,
Had watched his course and marked him for their own;
And now, from spangled caves and wave-flower haunts,
They sought his presence with an arrowy speed
That sheened the wavelets with phosphorent glow.
In shining bands they gathered round his form,

And lapped in sportive dalliance, they wound
Their watery arms around his bending neck;
Kissed with their clammy lips the beaded spray
Which dewed itself about his wave-wooed mouth,
And sung in rippling murmurs to his ears.
In trailing cerements of willowy sedge,
All foam-flake clustered round their limpid throats,
Their misty heads with water-lilies crowned,
The amorous Nereids all serenely came
Insidious, and with their icy touch
Cramped his limp limbs and charmed his strength
    away.

With sorrowing eyes he cast a lingering look
Where strayed the object of his heart's desire.
And, oh, the agony that shook his frame
And pierced his soul with sorrow-shafts of dole,
As on the beach he saw her kneeling form,
With outstretched arms and agonizing lips
Loud calling on the Virgin Queen of heaven
To save him for the sake of her dear Son.
Then ere he sunk to rise again no more,
With frenzied arm impelled with dying power
He broke the spell that drew him underneath,
And flung toward the spot where kneeled his love
The blue-hued flowers whose purchase was his life:
He sunk away into the waiting arms

Which folded him in many a chill embrace,
And bore him gently to the longing queen
Empalaced in the mystery of the lake,
While straying Zephyr wafted to the shore
The wingéd words which bubbled from his lips:
"Forget me not, sweet love, forget me not."

From soughing reed the startled heron sprung
On fluttering wings, and then, in circling swoop,
It sought its nest with angry boding cry.
The wild swans' matin flooded all the air
With music sweet as is the voice of song
When melting on the fervent soul of love;
Then all was silent, save a wave-sprite's sob,
As, pityingly, she sought the fatal spot,
Caught with her aqueous touch a straying flower,
And, gliding onward with a murmuring plaint,
Stole softly up the pebbled shore, and laid
It gently at the frantic maiden's feet;
Then shrunk away in timid pulsings, till
She sobbed herself to rest in tranquil depths,
And passed, in dream, to heaven's celestial sea.
With icy touch the maiden tenderly
Pressed to her pallid lips the conscious flower
Whose fragrant breath seemed burthened with the
    words,
"Forget me not, sweet love, forget me not."

The moonbeams sheened the waters, and the stars,
All cold, and shivering, tipped each tranquil wave
With starry crest, and gazed upon her form;
As, with self-chidings, eyes devoid of tears,
She swooned away into a death-like trance:
And there they found her, when, with measured
    strides,
The mailed retainers sought her straying feet,
Drawn there by nightingale, which, by her side,
On hazel spray, held sacred watch and sung
A mournful descant fraught with love and death.

On frame of boughs they placed her pulseless form,
Then sought with anxious steps the Castle's hall,
Through whose arched portals swelled loud cries of
    woe
From quivering lips, which spake a mother's grief,
As onward pressed the sire, an ancient Knight,
With stormy brows and wrath so ill-concealed
That they who followed after said he raved
And clutched the cross-hilt of his pond'rous brand,
And muttered imprecations fierce on those
Who dared to lead her unto danger's path,
Or harm a hair of her, his cherished pride.
But when he gazed upon her prostrate form
And wax-like features, pressed with seal of death,
He kneeled beside her on the dewy sward,

And with his trembling fingers' soft caress,
Drew from her forehead, chill, the clammy hair,
And with wan lips pressed to her bloodless cheek,
Told all his agony in blinding tears.

With solemn steps advanced St. Francis' monk.
His snowy locks, escaping from his cowl
Upon his breast, fell mingling with his beard;
And as he gazed upon the touching sight,
More mournful through the torches' ruddy glare,
He turned away his head and deeply sighed.
At his approach the sorrowing throng withdrew,
Crossing their breasts; and with a silent vow
Each vowed a gift unto his favorite saint
If he would interpose and save her life,—
For each one loved her more than passing well;
Because, full oft, like messenger from heaven,
When the red tide of onset had passed o'er,
With skilful hands she staunched their oozing gore;
And eased with herb and balm each smarting wound;
And poured sweet consolation in their ears;
And acts of kindness did to them and theirs
Until they loved her with a love as great
As manly hearts can yield to gentleness.

With kindly force the priestly healer turned
The grieving sire from his heart's delight;

Then plied with wondrous skill the leech's art;
And, aided by elixir of great fame,
Distilled from dews and precious essences,
And herbs of virtue, in chaste alembic,
By patient Wisdom's peerless alchemist,
In an enchanted cave of Araby:
Thence brought by Pope-blessed pilgrim-missioned
    monk
In crystal vial ta'en from Egypt's King
Entombed in heart of Sphinx-eyed pyramid,
Purged of all heathenness and demon arts,
And blessed to heaven and heaven's sweet designs,
By saint whose soul had won immortal bliss
Upon the flaming wings of martyrdom,—
Soft wooed her spirit to its earthly shrine
And stirred to breath the fountain of her life.
    *   *   *   *   *   *
But she ne'er smiled again. Though oft her praise
By joyous minstrel, bard, and knight was sung
At camp and court, and lance was lain in rest
And axe and brand in tourney and in field
Were raised to champion her as Beauty's queen;
Though princely suitors wooed with gifts and sighs,
And at her footstool bent the stubborn knee,
Unmoved she stood, a statue warm with life;
A mortal lily vow-betrothed to death,
Whose heart was wave-enshrined and ever sighed

The silent language of the mystic flower,—
"Forget me not, sweet love, forget me not."

As way-worn pilgrim from the sacred shrine
Bore on his bosom splinter of that cross
Upon whose frame the Son of Glory died,
So she, in gem-bossed locket, wore alway
The sad memento of undying love;
And ever to her yearning soul it sighed
The mournful burden of that dying voice,—
"Forget me not, sweet love, forget me not."

By day she heard but this, and oft in dreams,
When pitying Midnight kissed the world to sleep,
That dying plaint would haunt her restless couch,
And stir her to a deep and poignant grief.
Nor long she bore the life-consuming care;
For like a dear and welcome visitor,
Sweet Death, with gentle soothings, brought relief,
And tranced her spirit to its longed-for rest.

Amid the buried grandeur of the past
They laid her,—dust to dust,—and o'er her corse
Reared monumental pile, whose marble front
Was void of tribute from the artist's hand
Save sculptured flower upon a broken stem,
And underneath, the words, "Forget me not."

BALLAD OF COLIN CLOVER.

The eve was calm as mother Eve,
   As lovely and as fair,
When Colin "guessed" he'd take a walk
   And with it take the air.

High on his head his hat he hung;
   Raised Uncle Abel's cane;
Fired his meerschaum pipe, and strode
   With silence down Love's lane.

In stately rows above him rose
   Huge oak-trees gnarled and dense,
Which threw their limbs and shadows o'er
   The fence without offence.

His cheerful mind strayed while he strayed,
   And 'scaped his lips in glee
Which chorded in a sweet accord
   With Nature's minstrelsy.

His two-feet footsteps brought him to
   A fairy-haunted dell,
Between whose flower-spangled slopes
   A babbling streamlet fell.

Upon its marge he sat him down
   In contemplative mood,
Feeding his epicurean mind
   With intellectual food.

Then did his thoughts like birds fly through
   His sentimental brain,
And, lighting on his ambered lips,
   Poured forth this sad complain:

Glide on, ye gentle waters, glide
   Toward the palmy South,
And let the sorrow of your head
   Flow seaward through your mouth.

And as ye glance by mead and vale,
   Pregnate each wanton breeze
With embryonic murmurs of
   The far-resounding seas.

Kiss the sweet flowers whose perfumed heads
   Find on thy bosom rest,
And sigh when rude winds agitate
   The calmness of your breast.

Blush when the amorous glance of sun
   Invades thy bed, and sigh
When hungry trout, by artful Art,
   Is caught out on a fly.

Remirror hill, cot, mill, and trees
  Which breathe thy murmurings;
Reflect chaste Dian and her bow,
  With Saturn and his rings.

Thou'rt yet a rill, full soon to be
  A stream so deep and wide,
That on thy tide will steamers steam,
  And knaves and navies ride.

Then brought to bay, through gulf thou'lt stray,
  Till, lost in ocean's waves,
You'll answer to the breakers' whoop
  In melancholy staves.

Emblem of Time, whose solemn tide
  Bears life unto that sea
Whose waters lave the dreamy shores
  Of dread Eternity.

Thus mused he, till a piercing shriek
  Assailed his drowsy ears,
And stayed the current of his mind
  From running out in tears.

Thoughtless of gain, he gained his feet;
  Surveyed the country round;
Then left his survey, hat and cane,
  To find the source of sound.

Down in the meadow, where the mead
  Filled chin-shine buttercups,
He saw, beside a score of cows
  And gamb'ling lambs and pups,

A sight which icicled his blood
  And froze him to a pause,
While, like excited castanets,
  Chattered his sparse-haired jaws.

There, right before him, shrieking, flew
  On terror's frantic wings
A red-frocked maid, pursued by bull
  Propelled by hornet stings.

Like Ivanhoe when Beckie called,
  He hastened to her aid,
Whooping, like savage charging foe,
  To make the beast afraid.

"Oh, save me! save me!" gaspéd she;
  And staggering, in her charms,
Beside herself, unto his side,
  Wilted within his arms.

With pressman's strength he raised her form,
  Both arms about her waist;
Wasted no time, but, letter-like,
  Passed post and rail in haste.

On came the beast, with bellowing roar,
   A hundred rods behind,
His nasal organ furrowing grass,
   His caudal winnowing wind.

Ne'er did gay Matadore bull-bait,
   At Seville or at Cadiz,
A bull more moody in his mood,
   More frightful to the ladies.

Like the fierce Minotaur of Crete,
   He wanted human blood
To quench his quenchless ire and thirst,
   And salivate his cud.

Ah! 'twas a stirring sight to see
   The strivings of that race,
And mark the sweat-drops ooze, and course
   Down Colin's fear-flushed face;

To see his muscles on a swell;
   To eye his saucer eyes,
Which looked for all the world just like
   A calf's eyes at demise.

His "swallow-tail," like streamer, flew
   Back with the virgin's dress,
And Scrutiny, beneath, might see
   A signal of distress.

On, on he pressed. Unlike Lot's wife,
   He never looked behind,
But forward to the pinewood fence
   For which his spirit pined.

Like Alcibiades of eld,
   He strove to win the goal,
While, panorama-like, his life
   Flashed through his flutt'ring soul.

As he drew near to Safety's side,
   The beast drew near to him,
Until life's chance, like waning star,
   Paled dim, dim, dimmer, dim.

He gained the fence. Recruiting strength,
   He raised his senseless load,
And to old mother earth beyond
   His beauty he bestowed.

But ere, car-like, he jumped the rail,
   His bullship turned his steer,
Which brought him with a *queue-de-grace*
   On his defenceless rear.

Alas! poor Colin! Temperate youth!
   His prospect was forlorn!
He couldn't leave the cattle-bar
   Until he took a horn.

High in the air his father's heir
  Sped like a ball from gun,
And though 'twas time for stars to shine,
  Yet rising was the son;

Describing mathematic curves
  In summ'ry summerset,
He halted, like tired troops at night,
  'Mongst stones, sand, grass, and wet.

Stunned for the moment there he lay,
  An humble layman; he
Had nearly ended his career
  Without doxology.

His scattered senses one by one
  Resought his aching head;
On his reserve for strength he called,
  To raise him from his bed.

He rubbed his eyes; scratched rear; felt ribs;
  Then finger-ploughed his hair,
Till satisfied, though 'ware of earth,
  He was not earthenware.

Urged by a kindly sympathy,
  He kneeled upon the sand;
Without felonious intent,
  He took the maiden's hand.

Though cold as zero, yet the touch
  Thrilled Venus through his frame,
While Hymen fired his pulsing heart
  With love's ecstatic flame.

Enchantment held him with her spells,—
  Rome's saintliest anchorite
Had lost his hold on heaven had he
  Beheld the luscious sight.

Her hair in glossy ringlets fell
  Around a neck which rose
In queenly beauty from the sphere
  Where pleasure seeks repose.

Waxed alabaster seemed her face;
  Her voiceless lips apart,
Vied with the ivory of her teeth
  To captivate his heart.

Her arrowy form seemed like a Fay's;
  Figment of Artist's brain,—
Perfection all unconscious hid
  In folds of her delaine.

Alarmed, he raised a note of woe,
  And bore her to a bank
Which broke, or seemed to issue from
  A water-lilied tank.

With whining voice and water bright
   He bathed her on champaign,
And, sailor-like when ship makes port,
   He brought her to amain.

Life's necromancer, stealing through
   Her pearly veins so fair,
The lilies from her cheeks bewitched,
   And conjured roses there.

As timid sunbeam, coyish, peeps
   From cloud of summer skies,
So, from the windows of her soul,
   Peeped forth the glad surprise.

She moved, though 'twasn't moving day,
   And let a thrilling sigh
Elope with one from Colin's breast,
   And with it seek the sky.

Peach-blossom blushes frolicked o'er
   Her cheeks in rosy play,
While smiling smiles, in amorous mood,
   Beguiled his care away.

In voice attuned to peacock air,
   Ejaculated she,
"If 't hadn't been for you, kind sir,
   A spirit now I'd be.

"Ten thousand times ten thousand thanks
    To you I now impart,
Yet they can ne'er express to you
    The tribute of my heart.

"My name is Dolly Rural, sir,
    Squire Truly Rural's daughter;
I'm visiting my uncle Sam,
    Whose house stands by yon water.

"As I meandered down the lane,
    To gather home the cows,
I thought I'd take the nearest cut
    Across that critter's browse.

"You know the rest as well as me,—
    But, oh, good laud a massy!
I never dreamed Dad Grimshaw's bull
    Was so confounded sassy."

Dispelled the charm. Brave Colin's heart
    Fluttered like wind-stirred flag,
Causing his head and hand to give
    A sentimental wag.

His love oozed out. His ardor cooled
    Like melted sealing-wax;
He didn't feel like Eucherer feels,
    With ace and both the jacks.

But arm in arm he led her then
    Unto her uncle's gate;
Squeezed both her hands; thrice kissed "good-night;"
    Then left, though pressed to wait.

*   *   *   *   *   *

From that time forward, Colin was
    To Doll a welcome guest;
To please him she, with pa and ma,
    Essayed their level best.

And all the neighbors, far and near,
    From White's to Browns's patch,
Winked, while each to other said,
    "They'll surely make a match."

Now Sentiment would make two one,
    Likewise a lass, alas!
But Truth bids Honesty proclaim,
    It never came to pass.

For twelve months after,—more or less,—
    Bold Colin went his way;
Nor tarried long before he wed
    The rich young widow Grey.

And Dollie? She got "spliced" to Joe,—
   Dad Grimshaw's youngest son,—
Though often Colin and the bull
   Through her mind's eye would run.

Then all the gossips thereabouts,
   With shrug, and eyes aglow,
Mouthed, "Pooh! I knew they'd never mate,—
   I always told you so."

LOVE IN A PALACE.

SCENE.—*A Parlor in a lordly English mansion.*

In parlor, throned in royal state,
On velvet-cushioned tête-à-tête,
The lovers in a golden revery sat,
Exhausting all the luxury of chat,
And listening to the humming birds and bees
Whose buzzings floated through the waving trees.

Across the carpets wove with Orient dyes,
   Whene'er the gauzy curtains, zephyr-swayed,
Let in a straying sunbeam from the skies,
   They watched it come and go, and dusk, and fade,
Awhile the spirits of the odorous breeze
Danced lightly o'er the grand piano's keys.

Out through the open lattice, rose-embowered,
And honeysuckle-twined, and jasmine-flowered,
They saw, at foot of purple-mantled hills,
The river's glimmer,—heard the laugh of rills,
Till o'er an ocean of voluptuous bliss
Their fancies floated in a love-born kiss.

About them gold-set mirrors frescos showed,
   And imaged to their eyes rare works of art,
Which fed their minds with pleasure till they glowed
   And warmed to love, the language of the heart.

   Sweet "Genevieve," with saintly smile,
      Gazed on them from her framed recess,
   While near them, with her lips of guile,
      "Lucretia" wooed the fiend's caress.

   Brave "Boadicea," Briton's pride,
      Leaned near "Rowena," Hengist's bride;
   While o'er them rare "Godiva" rode,
      "In shower-bath of golden hair,"
   Through streets where breathless Silence strode;
      While peeping Tom, with blasted sight,
      Writhed in the agonies of night,
      And cursed the noontide's glare.

   There, in the pride of womanhood,
      On dizzy copestone of the tower,
   With scornful lips, "Rebecca" stood,
      Defying Guilbert's haughty power.

   Anear them, framed elaborately,
      Stern "Canute" sat beside the sea,
   Bidding the savage white-crest waves
      Retire, quiescent, to their caves.

Beyond, crazed Lear's emaciate form,
   His white hairs flowing with the wind,
Defied, on heath, the "naughty" storm,
   And poured his curses on mankind.

On other hand, by windmills' mote
Rode Sancho and brave Don Quixote;
And, as companions, "Hudibras
   And Ralpho," when they first rode forth
In warlike guise and stained cuirass,
   To scourge the "Godless" of the North.

Before them, loving "Romeo
   And Juliet" in a fond embrace,
Shunning the moon's effulgency,
Stood in the dusk of secrecy,
Their fluttering spirits all aglow,
   With heart to breast and cheek to face;

And on them they both fixed their gaze
And dreamed the love of other days,
      Until, in warm caress,
Like Zephyr wantoning in flower,
In bliss they breathed "a vast half-hour"
      Amid the silentness.

The marble Venus by their side
   Approved their rapturous bliss,
While Cupid, with a lover's pride,
Seemed light and airily to glide
   His Psyche loved to kiss.

Attendant Fays, delirious with the sight,
Floated upon the crystal waves of light;
And music, disenthralled from prison strings
Of jewel-fretted harp; then,.folding wings,
They sighed a rapturous melody,
Caught from the pearl-lipped shells of sea,
While fretful one, æolianly,
Whispered, "Straying honey bee,
Away! it seemeth ill to thee
In a parlor thus to seek
Rosy bloom of virgin cheek.
Reckless, teasing fly, astray,
From her presence stay away!

Death, and that, too, suddenly,
From Love's hand will come to thee,
If thou, wanton, chance to rest
On the chasteness of her breast,
Or from chalice of her lip
Undertake to filch a sip

Of Elysian ecstasy
Nurtured there for Love, not thee,
Which he guardeth jealously."

Then agitated sylphs of bloom,
Swinging censers of perfume,
Athrough the silence of the room,
Chaunted, as they breathed their sighs,
And felt the influence of their eyes,
"Oh, essence of deliciousness!
Oh, heaven of earthly happiness!
See! see! they drink!—how dreamily!—
The wine of love pressed from the grapes
Which purple with their joys the capes
Laved by the waves of Arcadie!
Cease, throbbing heart, and list Love's feet
Fall, tinkling, to the luscious greet.
See!—bubbling, upward floats a kiss,
Freighted with sighs and hallowed bliss;
Waft it, oh, waft it, spirits, straight
To Dian's court by heaven's gate."

Evanished they with faint melodious sighing,
When from an oleander's scent came flying
A wingèd voice, which carolled amorously
To the soft flutes of Fairy minstrelsy,—

"Warbling sprite of gilded bars,
Save your warble for the stars;
Locust, cease your grating drone,
Grasshopper, your monotone;
Katydid, your sad complaint
Keep for ear of pitying saint;
Alabastered Niobe,
Wed to fountain cunningly,
Dry your eyes and cease to weep
While you croon yourself to sleep;
For ye but disturb the rest
Of Love, who loveth silence best."

Then from the hills of Echo, far remote,
A still-born whisper, halcyonly, did float;
And, floating, murmured so delicious clear,
That Fancy caught these words on raptured ear:
"Zephyr, fold your sultry wing
And cease your airy gossiping;
Myth of air and elf of breeze,
Curb your tipsy jollities;
Mite of dusk and mote of beam,
Vain Ephemera of gleam,
Strangle your hilarity
And for the moment cease to be;
Revellers in Thought's domain,
All your gypsyings restrain,

Lest ye, with concerted breath,
Bring to an untimely death
The single thought which doth obtain
Possession of the lover's brain."

Imagination, with a sigh
As fond as mother's lullaby,
Spake through the marble lips of Venus, nigh
The pair, whose glowing souls absorbed in sky,
Heard neither knock nor telephone's soft cry:
"Proud magnolia, your scent
Self-absorb, and somnolent
Poppy-Peris, stay awhile
The subtle glamour of your guile;
Pansied heart's-ease, your vain sighing
Cease, lest start ye Love's thoughts flying;
Wilding Fancy, floating free
Through the mind's tranquillity,
Siesta take ye now, nor call
Precious memories from pall;
Weird Enchantment, work the spell
Which Experience knoweth well;
Sunbeam, stay your glittering,—
Each and every sound take wing;
Bird, fount, flower, thought, and gleam,
Conspire to sweeten Love's young dream."

Thrilled to her bosom's core, her hand,
  All love-a-tremble, then he pressed
  To his pale lips and pulsing breast;
As if at conjurer's command,
Upbubbled from her well of sighs
Into the sunlight of her eyes,
Her beamy soul, which, sparkling, fell
  In showers on his kneeling form,
Like subtleness of magic spell
  On passions rapturously warm:
And then she breathed the witchery
Of love's delicious sorcery,
While he, like captive bird when beauty flings
Her jewelled fingers o'er its prisoned wings,
All trembling whispered to her ravished ear
Th' impassioned words Love ever hopes to hear:

  "Wilt thou be mine, love? Deign reply!
  Speak, dearest, speak, else will I die!
  Charm of my soul,—my amulet!
  Consent to be my Juliet.
  Speak, darling, speak, my soul, in gloom,
  Impatient waits to hear its doom:
  Life of my life,—love's violet!
  Oh, say thou'lt be my Juliet!"

Cupid, enraptured, whirled in ecstasy
And effervesced champagneously,

Frisking in pantomime; and as he boomed
He twanged his bow, his wanton shaft replumed,
Smiling the while a mirth-provoking smile,
Delicious as the subtlety of guile;
And in delirium of joy, his dart
He pointed *point-blank* at his mother's heart;
But she ne'er stirred nor heeded him at all.
Mutely entranced, she leaned from pedestal,
Gazing with marble gaze on mirrored wall
At her own image, which, imbued with life
By ardent sun-god, watched the amorous strife
Pervading, with her influence, the pair,
Absorbing all the wine-bouquet of air.
Sighing ambrosially and chaste
As, spirit-urged, about her virgin waist
He wound his eager arm, voluptuously,
And drew her to himself,—Divinity,
Which pilots Love o'er Passion's lustful sea
And safely harbors it in chastity;
Spirit, whose cohorts guard the citadel
Where Modesty and Purity do dwell,
Be on alert! 'Tis now Fate weaves the spell
Which wafts the soul to bliss, or warps to hell;
And you, celestial Harmonist, set free
The enambered soul of heavenly Harmony,
And bid her in sweet dream of melody
Sigh to the mind a mystic rhapsody,

And to the mind reveal where, of lust shorn,
Passion expires and guileless love is born:
Yea, to our blunted senses demonstrate,—
   As palpable as light unto the eye,
   Or mist when mingling with the morning sky,—
The blending of two souls, decreed by Fate
To pass united through this mortal state,
   And through the changes of eternity.

Exuded from the fragrant atmosphere,
As noiselessly as oozes Pity's tear,
All daintily arrayed in sundusk gear,
A troop of wayward fancies, exquisite,
Who, charging all the air with subtle wit,
Conjured to smile the Demon of despair,
And charmed the wrinkles from the brow of Care;
And with the Fancies came, bewitchingly,
A tawny rout of truant Phantasies,
Who, mixing with the teeming Atomies
Which haunt the tissues of the Poet's brain,
And thrill the soul with Love's ecstatic pain,
Filled with their presence the enamoured air
Which wrapped in warm embrace the happy pair,
   To feast, if might be, on the dulcet sound
   Made by the expected word from hearts profound,
The golden answer to Love's ardent prayer.

Nestling within her mind, like fledgling bird
   Loath to depart from mother's fond caress,
   Where all is loving care and tenderness,—
The magic Word remained, nor breathed, nor stirred,
Though freighted with a vast, sweet, fierce desire
To gain the wooer's heart and quench its amorous fire.
Entangled in bewilderment it dozed,
Awhile the portals of her mind were closed;
Till, spirit-stirred, as star-beam in eclipse
Struggles to gain the day, it struggled to her lips
While lovingly her dainty finger-tips,
Unconscious, trifled with th' emblazoned crest
Which flashed and glittered from his throbbing breast;
And there it perched in blushing ecstasy,
An airy waif on mount of Mystery,
Dreaming irradiant dreams unutterable,
Wishing that naught but death might break the spell;
Fondly desiring, yet coyish to betray,
The secret of her soul, shrined in its heart, that gave
       the maid away.
Then, like an incense from the altar, where
The contrite spirit pleads with fervent prayer,
Athrough the casements of the lordly room,
Insinuatingly evolved a rare perfume,
Which, stifling all the odors of the bloom,
Filled each existence with a rare delight,
Provocative of earthly appetite,

And crooned to mind of that fair realm away
Beyond the blissful valleys of Cathay,
Where Alph, the sacred river, purling, runs
O'er diamond sands, beneath proud Kubla's suns,
Where, pleading, bow Urania's vestal nuns,
And at Devotion's shrine evoked the god of fire
To grant each devotee their heart's desire;
And with th' exhilarating fragrance came,
Like Fay exhaled from bog-sprite's lambent flame,
A wee lithe figure, garbed in spotless white,
With flowing curls by amber witches spun
From the mild radiance of the waning sun,
Whose glimmer, shimmering through the curtain's lace,
Bopeeped with smiles, which, bee-like, swarmed his face,
And aureoled his brows, till dazzled sight
Might deem him a beatified delight
By Mercy's gracious will from heaven sent,
To be to man a sweet encouragement.
Urged by sly Puck, who, since the peep of day
Sporting with Ariel and the culprit Fay,
Had chased Illusions round the coral shores
Of Madagascar and the bright Azores;
And who, from home of wind, on highest cliff
Of sun-ray-crowned and cloud-girt Teneriffe,
Had flashed on wings of light to England's coast,
Ere dying day had shadowed to a ghost;
And bent on mischief, sped in haste away
To that fair mansion innocently gay,

Where, 'scaping guardian Love's elusive snare,
He sought the presence of the loving pair,
Toying a moment with her wealth of hair,
And then found lodgement in the urchin's mind,
Which filled he with the whimsies of the wind.
Silent, as flow of light through the effulgency,
O'er Oriental velvets tip-toed he;
Now hidden by this statue, now that chair,
He glided onward, like a shape of air,
Until, by screen of Arras tapestry,
Which portrayed Cœur-de-Leon's chivalry,
He stood, and, chuckling with boycotted glee,
Gazed on the lovers steeped in ecstasy.

Love's tongue, delirious, was quivering to utter
The golden word, when mouse-like squeak and flutter
Disturbed the silence, and on lover's ear
Fell with a nervous jar. Again, more clear,
As like a shaft of light from Dian's bow,
Sped from the screen, with eyes and cheeks aglow,
The urchin, shouting most hilariously,
"Oh, Auntie Gertrude! Ha, he, he!
I saw him kiss you! Come now, come to tea;
Her Highness, gloomy grand and silently,
Impatient waits. Oh my, you needn't blush!
Your tell-tale rosy face is all a-flush!

Ma telephoned you thrice; she did, ay, thrice!
And I was sent to usher you in twice;
But then I came at my own sovereign will,—
Oh my! how cross you look! I can't be still!
Ha, ha! how close he hugged you! He! he! he!
Don't linger longer, do come out to tea!
Aunt Bess once said,—ah, now you smile!—
Love is but wind,—all lovers' words are guile,—
You needn't curl your lips at me in scorn;—
Or look like House that Jack built's maid forlorn;
For pa told ma, last night, he only wished
That coming wedding might be quickly dished;
Or, if it did transpire, he hoped the groom
Had more to live on than his helmet's plume,—
What 'tis he meant, I'm sure I do not know.
Oh, dearest aunt, your face is like the snow;
And yours, my lord, with savage flame's aglow."

The encaged mock-bird, urged to mimicry,
Disturbed the stillness with rude mockery,
And saucy parrot, stirred from revery,
Shrieked, "Auntie Gertrude! He, he, he!
I saw him kiss you! Come now, come to tea."
As from the lawn a peacock, haughtily,
Spread pridefully his tail, for all to see;
While from the paddock, by the greenwood tree,
An amorous donkey brayed vociferously.

THE ENCHANTERS; OR, THE DANCE OF DEATH.

On the swarded slope of a sylvan lake
Which spread like a mirror, without a break
Of ruffling ripple or foamy flake;

In the sombre haze of a castled steep,
O'er whose crags the shadows had ceased to creep,
And with the coy breezes had gone to sleep

On campus where neighbors, to 'scape the heat,
Assembled to feast, or tipple, and greet,
Or chase the fleet moments with twinkling feet;

All shrivelled and wrinkled, gaunt, sallow, and gray,
In tattered garments of fustian stood they
Beside the cathedral, and carolled a lay.

Whence came they, neighbor? But none of them knew
Whether exhaled from the air, like the dew,
Or whether like pestilent toadstools they grew.

And their grisly dog, with his eyes of crime,
And snarling fangs!—did he ooze from the slime?
Or glide, like a snake, from the reeking grime?

The harper's fingers, aged, weary, and thin,
Waxed motionless; and the garrulous din
Died out with the sigh of the mandolin.

The expectant throng stood in breathless awe,
As out from his bosom they saw him draw
A grinning skull with a chattering jaw.

Then she, in the face of the dazed crowd, shook
Her tambourine with a menacing look,—
Hooted from minster the owl, cawed the rook!

As twilight flooded his Nazarene beard,
A dirge he chaunted, sad, solemn, and seared,
And up in the gray air the skull he reared,

Where, unsupported, it shook and quivered;
From its eyeless sockets a fierce light rivered;—
With fear the astonished villagers shivered,

As out of its brainless hollow it shook
Its skeleton frame. Then the color forsook
Each crimsoned cheek, and wild waxed each look.

E'en the barefoot friar, from his revery,
Arose from his vigil 'neath headman's tree,
And with pale lips conned o'er his breviary;

While simple Fritz turned his addled head,
Crossed his throbbing breast with an insane dread,
And into the gloom of the cloister fled.

Then slow to the "thrum" of the tambourine,
With a ghoulish grin and a vamp'rish mien,
The live-death waltzed round th' enchanted green.

Like the sea-fire glowed its clattering bones,
The gales, as they touched them, expired in moans,
And the ghost of the eve sighed in monotones.

The frail flowers withered beneath its tread,
The sensitive grasses their greenness shed,
And the fragrance of clover escaped and fled.

The evening star, with a tremulous shimmer,
As it shone through the haze, waned dim and dimmer,
And the red moon rose with portentous glimmer.

While maidens shrunk from its presence and sighed,
Each matron clung to her husband's side,
And the children hid in their bosoms and cried.

E'en the saintly seer of the village shook
With an aguish dread, as he caught its look,
And kissed devoutly his relic and book.

In unison with his tremulous hand
The Enchanter waved his magical wand,
When, like a trained cobra on Indian strand,

The Elf-death swayed with the dreamy motion
Of sullen wave of an angered ocean,
And began to dance with a fierce emotion.

Round and around like an air-whirl it flew,
Till th' encrimsoned atmosphere burnéd blue,
And painted each face with a ghastly hue.

Then quick the Enchantress, surged to and fro,
Made her soul with a thrill through her music flow,
With fascination her eyes all aglow.

Then the white-fanged dog, near his master's feet,
Pawed the torrid earth, and, cruel as sleet,
Growled fierce as a thwarted tiger in heat.

And then, while he bristled his wiry hair,
His glances flashed through the lurid air,
While he sneaked and couched, like a lion in lair,

By the side of the crone. Faster, still faster,
The Elf-death whirled round the Sphinx-eyed master,
Whose features glittered like alabaster.

The affrighted airs through his bleached bones hissed
Like angered asps, and the poisonous mist
Rose from the ground with a sinuous twist

That spiralled each bone with a frantic ire,
Till it clomb to and haloed its skull with fire,
Which shone like the wraith of a funeral pyre.

Beneath the tread of its clattering feet
The lush turf shrivelled, like sun-scorched wheat,
And the flint-sands glowed with a fervent heat.

The wine-guzzling, mailed retainers, three,
Who unhelmed sat in the grapery
Of "The Margrave's Arms," steeped in revelry,

Their janglings ceased, and in wild dismay
Upset their horn cups, and with lips ash-gray
To the Mother of Jesus essayed to pray.

And the jerkined lout who the troopers served,
Aghast with fear, from his balance swerved,
Dropped his goat-skin flagon, and sunk unnerved.

E'en the valorous burgomaster shook
Like a ghost-scared child, and his schnapps forsook,
As he fainted away 'neath its fiendish look.

Shriller the voice of the sorceress grew,
Till it pierced, like sorrow, each dazed brain through,—
Swifter and swifter the live-death flew.

Its white arms, like flails, the ambient air
Threshed, till it shone with a torturing glare
And electrified the Enchanter's hair,

Till it rose from his scalp a sheaf of light,
And luminous made the shuddering night,—
Each face grew green and ashen and white.

Then the hideous hag, with a frantic bound,
Shot, like a shaft of hell, from the ground,
And whirled in a flame-mist the live-death round.

Twirling, she shrieked a horrible stave,
With blasphemy charged, and full of the grave,
Like the shriek of demon beneath hell's wave.

Then her tambourine, with a sudden flare,
Evanished in smoke, and into thin air,
But its goblin music still lingered there.

Still lingered there, while plain to the view
Her leprous flesh turned a scarlet hue,
And in blood-red sparks from her gaunt frame flew,

Till all of her fleshless bones, absolved
From the dross of earth, like a star, dissolved,
Around the Enchanter's form revolved.

Then Katharina, the nine-months' bride,
The beloved of all, each villager's pride,
So tender-hearted and heavenly-eyed,

From the sweet retreat of her husband's breast
Passed in a swoon to her blissful rest,
And the unborn soul of her babe caressed.

But bound by the spell was the crowd, and dazed,
That it little heeded the shriek, half crazed,
Which the anguished soul of the bridegroom raised.

Nor more did it heed the dull mutterings
Of the storm, nor the bird-wing flutterings,
Nor the watch-dogs' querulous utterings,

Nor mark the sough of the lake, wind-stirred,
Nor the ominous "hoot" of Minerva's bird,
Which flashed through the gloom as if fury-spurred,

Nor the bleat of sheep, nor the bellow of kine,
Nor the snort of the stallion, 'neath cloven pine,
Nor the shrill, sharp grunt from the herd of swine.

Then the snarling dog-ghoul, with hideous scowl,
To the parched earth crouched, with a sullen growl,
Which rose in a scale to an angry howl,

Upflew like a fiend of insanity,
All blotched with the plague-spots of leprosy,
At the breast of the flesh-covered mystery,

And tore therefrom, with his fangs and claws,
The quivering heart, which, with gnash and gnaws,
He carried away in his blood-stained jaws.

With a cry like the wail of a spirit lost,
The heartless Enchanter his wand uptossed,
When it changed to a wyvern as white as frost,

Which winged to a crimsoned mist, which then
Arose from the lake, like a death-light from fen,
And flashed, with a hiss, through the weird wolf's glen;

While he, with his phosphorent flesh ablaze,
Sped meteor-like through the pestilent haze,
In pursuit of the dog in his devious ways.

Whirled fiercely the live-death and fleshless witch
Through an air as murk as the fumes of pitch,
Round wizard and dog, which, like maddened bitch,

THE ENCHANTERS; OR, THE DANCE OF DEATH.

Shook the bloody foam from his jaws, as his hair
Shot from his hide through the luminous air,
Like needles of fire through furnace's glare.

Then his rotten flesh dissolved to a dew,
And that to a upased vapor, which flew
On the wings of the gales, the gray airs through.

But his basilisk eyes and his blood-red tongue
To their chalky sockets and jawbones clung,
Like consumption's leech to a putrid lung.

Amid the glamour, the villagers gazed
With a vacant stare; and, with brains bedazed,
Followed the three, aghast and amazed.

Moaned the wind-stirred lake like a world in pain;
Groaned the shuddering trees, quaked the palsied plain;
Surged the rock-ribbed hills like a storm-tossed main;

Flowed from cathedral, through window and spire,
The groaning of organ, the wail of the lyre,
And "Dies Iræ" of sorrowing choir;

While, from pillared aisles and from many a cell,
Cowled monks emerged, and with torch, and with bell,
Sought the green by the castled citadel.

Dolorously tolled from belfry a knell
From whose waves of sound wingéd heralds of hell,
Shook from their fire-plumed pinions a spell

Which fell on the monks, as a withering blight
Falls on the bloom of the fields by night;
Quaked they with dolor and blanched they with fright

As the great fierce eyes, all purple and bleared,
Into their souls through their dazed eyes peered,
While, fading in night, they mockéd and jeered,

And shrieked, as from ivy-walled Abbey there came,
Like visions of light through the blue of the flame,
The white-robed nuns, who, with loud exclaim,

Besought the Virgin to soften the ire
Of the Holy One in His wrath of fire,
And accord His will to their weak desire.

The flitting frames of the dancing three
Ceased their gyrations, and amorously
Clasped their glowing hands, while deliriously

They danced the witching Walpurgis of Death,
Throbbed the great heart of Nature; winds held their
    breath,
And afar the "Wild Huntsman" swept over the heath.

But faster, still faster and faster they flew,
Till their weird forms were blent; and, like cyclone, they drew
In the whirl, one by one, of the crowd. And then grew

More frantic the dance,—monk, nun, burger, and crone,
Maid, soldier, and child, with a desolate groan,
Flashed fast through the gloom to the music of moan.

Then the gorgoned dog, charged with maniac ire,
Sprung at the throat of child, matron, and sire,
And bore them to earth, which, with sulphurous fire,

Shuddered and heaved with an earthquake spasm,
Which fissured the hills with a horrible chasm,
And convulsed the lake to a wild phantasm.

The brazen skies flashed to an intense glare,
Which paralyzed all the enchanted air,
Till, awakened to life by a simoon's fierce blare,

It charged with malignance the atmosphere,
Which stupefied all with sepulchral fear,
That froze at their fountains each woful tear.

Then out of the storm-dazzled hazes came,
On fiery charger, as scarlet as shame,
The Angel of Death, with his sword of flame;

And then as the dog, in his furious wrath,
Covered with victims his desolate path,
Smote them as David, the giant of Gath.

Through the lurid vapors, their wraiths, all askew,
Fled shrieking and praying. Then out of the yew,
Midst blackness of darkness, a firebolt flew,

Like a blighting curse, to the banquet hall
Of the lordly castle, whose turrets so tall
O'ershadowed the bounds of the village wall,

And then as the princely Margrave arose
From his daised throne, and made loud propose
To vassal and guest, who, in tabled rows,

Steeped in wassail, sat in the flambeau's glare,
With courtly graces, and maudlin stare,
To drink joy and health to the new-born heir.

Blared trumpet, clashed cymbals, and minstrelsy,
Shook the antique rafters with roisterous glee,
And the fool's bells jangled with revelry.

Chimed silver tankard and goblet of gold
Euphoniously; but, ere palates could mould
The wine to their taste, the thunder-shell rolled

Above them and burst. With the new-born's name
On their shrivelled lips, 'neath the lambent flame,
Sunk blasted and withered each stalwart frame.

Leaped, like vaulting demons from Fury's glance,
The subtile fluid from sword's point and lance,
While on harness of battle it sparkled in dance,

And wreathed with red horrors the trophies of war;
Rare tapestries, arts; then out of each door
And embrasure it surged with a terrified roar.

By spirit hands swayed, the alarum bell
Of the castle uttered a dolorous knell,
And the wind-torn banner and pennons fell,

As copestone of tower went crashing through
To the vaulted hall, where, with chosen few,
The mother and babe, on mattress of rue,

Reclined. God of mercy, avert! Do not slay!
Pity!—Crushed, bleeding and mangled they lay,—
No absolution! Nor time there to pray.

As a tempest-tossed bark, bereft of rudder,
Struck by fierce blast, careers with wild shudder,
So the bolt-struck earth quaked, like bee-stung udder.

Then, from chancel, crypt, and sarcophagus,
From church-yard and death-field miraculous,
With groanings and chatterings clamorous,

The dusky shades of departed men
Emerged, like illusions from haunted glen,
And flashed into dance on the 'wildered ken.

With loathful antics and grotesque bound,
They waltzed the flaming Death-Angel around,
While their murmurings startled the dim profound.

Quickened to life, those by Death's cur laid low
All fleshless uprose; and, with frames all aglow,
They joined in the dance to the music of woe.

The angered skies glowed with the intense glare
Of a meteor-star. And the powers of air
Deliriously shrieked, as with flaming hair

They fiend-like flashed, with an imped grimace,
And illumed an instant the dimness of space,
Then fell they to nothing, as angels from grace.

Then the blazing clouds whirled down with fierce roar
To the seething lake, raised its waves, and bore
Them beyond the bounds of the quaking shore,

And burst o'er the village; wall, mansion, and tower,
Cathedral, and mart, succumbed to its power,—
Until nothing remained of stone, tree, or flower.

E'en the blasted walls of the castle fell
With a crash that startled the Cæsar of hell,—
Floated the dancers through valley and dell.

*　*　*　*　*　*　*

Peeped red, through the rifts of the storm, a star,
While echoed from heavenly gates ajar
A trumpet's blast. Flashed a radiant bar

Across the skies. Then the wild dance of death
Ceased, and the dream-gendered shadows of breath
Died out,—so the black-letter legend saith.

EPISODES IN THE LIFE

OF

ALLIEGUNDABAGO,

GREAT CÆSAR AND ATOTARHO

OF THE

ALGONQUIN ARASAPHAS.

A nation of copper-skinned humans, who, in prehistoric years, held undisputed sway over all the lands stretching from the river Hochelaga (St. Lawrence) to the Gulf of Mexico, and from the Atlantic Ocean to the Rocky Mountains, the same having the seat of their empire planted above the present site of Philadelphia, their grand council lodge covering the spot (then an eminence) now occupied by the new city buildings, at the intersection of Market and Broad Streets.

ALLIEGUNDABAGO:

EPISODE No. 1. THE MASTODON.

EPISODE No. 2. OFF CAPE COD.

EPISODE No. 3. A DREAM HE DREAMED.

ALLIEGUNDABAGO.

MAJESTIC was his form. His height
Exceeded Europe's men of might;
And in his elbows, neck, and knees,
Reposed the strength of Hercules.
His hair, as dark as starless night,
Was gloss as peacock anthracite,
And flowed, in gleaming falls of jet,
Down to his breech-clout's belteret.
On either side, from high cheek-bone,
   His massive forehead swelled and rose,
   Above a wide, heroic nose,
Which breathed on thin lips cold as stone.
Athrough his voice a torrent flowed
Of words which eloquently glowed;
While from his eyes, like radiant gems,
   Where passion's fiery lightnings slept,
   The living brightness flashed and leapt,
And played like glint of diadems.
Each cheek disclosed, in vermeil red,
A tattooed snapping-turtle's head,—
   The totem of his race,
   And symbol of his place;—

And on his brawny breast, blue seared,
A rampant rattlesnake upreared
   In striking attitude.
Around his burly neck was geared
   A snake-skin necklace rude,
Worked o'er with fangs from serpents' jaws
And eagle scalps and grizzlies' claws
   And scolloped figures, crude.
His pow'rful arms were armleted
With dragon scales, worked on in red,
   And tawny belzerene.
His pliant wrists were braided round
With wampum bracelets set and wound
   With pearls of ocean's sheen.
Drooped from his waist a philibeg
Of deerskin wrought by Winnipeg,
   Of bloody Arkansaw.
His sinewy legs were buff'lo-thonged;
His supple ankles clasped and tonged
   With hooks from vultures' claw.
His noble feet were moccasined
With leather lightning-tanned and skinned
   From pterodactyl's back.
When on the war-path's sinuous trail
He swept along like angered gale,
   His limbs were smutched with black.

And from his scalp-lock's crimsoned crest
A Phœnix' plume, in wild unrest,
  Dallied on breeze's wing.
Of polished hickory was his spear,
Tipped with antler bone of deer,
  Scraped keen as hornet's sting.
An iron-wood club, with knotted head,
Spiked with an elk-horn, sanguine red,
  His stalwart shoulders decked.
Hung from his body-belt of hide
Obsidian knife, and axe beside,
  With scarlet feathers flecked.
His matchless bow, of bone and ash,
  Swung at his back with birch-bark quiver,
Held by a crystal-beaded sash,
  Which gleamed in sun like beam-kissed river.
His pipe, of redstone carved, was worn
With his tobacco-box of horn,
Anear his pouch of sugared corn.

  His skill was wonderful with hatchet;
None ever born of flesh could match it;
And with the knife and war-club, he
  His equal never lived to see.
The war-path's devious ways he trod,
  Like an avenging heathen god.

The conflict was his chief delight;
He revelled in the air of fight;
  And, like the steed of battle,
He snuffed the foeman from afar,
And onward dashed, like Jove-hurled star,
  'Mid noise of gong and rattle.
When ambuscade his lines unrolled,
His deeds were awful to behold;
And when surprise or grim mêlée
Coaxed his plumed braves from rock or tree,
Hell clapped its hands and screamed with glee.
Amid the storm of blows he stood,
Like giant oak 'mid sapling wood,
Defying thunderbolt and wind,
And all the rage of human kind.
His followers, like tidal flood,
Surged o'er the land, knee-deep in blood,
And worked his sanguinary will,
From Mexico to Quebec's hill.
Where'er he raided, sovereign wrath
Whirled, like a cyclone, on its path;
And grim destruction, wrack, and death,
Lived in the tempest of his breath.

But in his grisly presence, there
Rang horrid whoop; rose frightened hair;
Shone scarlet scalps; gleamed bosoms bare;

Gushed blood; oozed brains; flew shrieking
        ghosts;
Hacked limbs; and flames of torture-posts;
Fell mournful showers of maidens' tears,
Shed for their grandames 'paled on spears;
There raged the battle's din, and hum
Of the weird powwow's tum-e-tum;
The blaze of wigwam, and the glare
Of burning forests; maize-fields bare
Of pumpkins, squashes, beans, and corn,—
Naught there but orphans, all forlorn,
And spirits of the blasted heath,
Sans everything but skull and teeth;
Triumphant chaunt of victory;
The craven's shriek of agony;
The laugh and dance of revelry;
The squawk of squaws; dog's yelp, and whine;
The taunt of death-song; grunt of swine,
And all else in the category
Of roaring, first-class, Indian story.

EPISODE No. 1.

THE MASTODON:

The skeleton of which was found in a marsh near Newburgh, N. Y., and set up by Dr. Warren, of Boston. It now stands in the British Museum, and is the wonder of all who behold it.

WITH Shackamaxon of the Oaks,
Hunting for "spuds" and artichokes,
While cracking heels and nuts and jokes,
   By falls of Manayunk;
They paused a moment, in their glee,
'Neath Conshohocken's council-tree
   To sing "Coc-ca-che-lunk,"
When on their startled hearing fell,
Like whizz of ball or burst of shell
   On sleeping camp at night,
A dolorous roar, surcharged with hell,
Which, like an icy terror, fell
   And chilled their souls with fright;
And when, in fulness of dismay,
They sought their feet to run away,
   They scarce could stand upright;
And, ere they'd time to launch a pun
Or 'jaculate Jack Robinson,

    Through morning's dewy light,
    Flashed on their 'wildered sight
An earthquake-breeding mastodon,
With eyes as fierce as noonday's sun,
    And trunk of ghostly white,
Which swift as ball from cannon sent,
For hapless Shackamaxon went,
    And 'paled him on its tusk;
Then flung him high and high and higher,
With nostrils snorting mists of fire,
    Odorous as fetid musk;
And when the body reached the blue,
Like sunbeamed haze escaped from view,
    It never more was seen;
But ere the brute its eye-balls rolled,
Great Alliegundabago, bold,
    Achieved the trampled green;
And, coming to himself, with heed
His unstrung bow with cautious speed
    He strung as quick as wink;
Then, taking to a neighboring oak,
Which offered shelter from the poke
    Of the fierce creature's tusk,
He fitted arrow to the gut,
And aimed it at the shifting butt,
    With ne'er in eye a blink;

And while the quarry made its mark,
Tore from the trees the waveless bark,
   Like squaw from corn the husk,
And filled the palpitating air
With fury, branches, leaves, and scare,
   Let the keen arrow fly;
Clear through the shivering form it sped,
Like bolt by angered storm-cloud shed,
   Out flew it through an eye,
And in the heart of distant tree,
Which swayed and creaked with agony,
   Its quivering force was spent.
Down dropt the head and drooped the tail,
Like bellied sheet bereft of gale,
   On shivering knees all sunk;
And as the beast breathed foam and gore
In mist and steam behind, before,
   With insane fury drunk,
Swelled from its breast a bellowing roar,
Like swell from waves on bouldered shore,
   Which surged the flowing breeze;
The sweet-tooth bear and timid deer
Stopped in their tracks o'ercome with fear,—
   Shuddered th' affrighted trees.
Great birds, on wing clear out of sight,
Swooned in the ruffled air from fright
   And fluttered to the ground.

Hill, stream, and valley groaned aloud,
And threw their echoes to the cloud
  Which filled the blue profound;
And, like a great collapsed balloon,
The wilted cloud in dreamy swoon
  Of mist and rain came down.
Alliegunda, from his tree
Sprung forward cool, collectedly,
  And grasped his eager spear
  From the great rock anear;
And as the frantic creature rose,
He put his body in a pose,
  And thrust into its ear
Th' elastic weapon, from his weight,
Sprung, like a catapult, and straight
  Into the vaulted blue,
He vaulted, like an acrobat,
From off a spring-board's swaying flat,
  Whooping his war "bo-hoo!"
"Oh, for a lodge in wilderness!"
Oozed from the lips of his distress.
  The bear-god heard his cry,
And lodged him in a buttonwood,
Which, like a sylvan giant, stood
  Conveniently nigh.
And there by nape of neck he hung,
The gnarled and naked limbs among,

An agitated Jack,
Until the limbs unloosed their hold
And let him fall, all fear and cold,
   Astride the monster's back.
In panic haste the monster flew
Like Satan from St. Dunstan's view,
   A whirlwind on its course.
While he, like waif upon the main,
   As through the country it went bounding,
Glued to its hair, as Fear to rein,
   Awhile its bellowing roar was sounding,
   Like neigh of Death's pale horse.
Goaded by spur of fear and pain,
It sped across the open plain,
   And midst the laughing trees;
O'er swollen creeks and rivers wide,
It strode with bold majestic stride,
   Which stirred to gale the breeze.
Hills ticklybendered 'neath its tread,
Which shook from earth the bones of dead
   Companions of the mole.
The basking snakes squirmed to their dens
Among the brambled rocks and fens;
   The scared fox sought his hole,
And each wild creature, with raised head,
Stood petrified with awful dread,
   And filled the air with dole.

Fierce hunters after flesh and bone,
The sneaking wolf and lynx alone
   Led by the scent of blood,
A yelping, snarling, howling pack,
Pressed by the thousands on its track
   A living, moving flood.
And Alliegundabago shook
With ague when he cast his look
Down in the maize-field vale below
And saw the wigwams of his foe,—
   The Mohawks of the vale,—
And when he heard their whoops and cries,
Which split the air and rent the skies,
   A moment he turned pale,
But ere 'twas given him to think,
Within the twinkle of a wink,
   With bloody snort and whack,
The monster dashed 'mid the wigwams,
And slashed and smashed them with its flams,
   Followed by howling pack.
Distraction seized the Mohawk crew,
On terror's outstretched wings they flew,
   To hide 'mong rocks and hills;
Warriors and chief and medicine,
Papoose, squaw, maid, with screeching din
   And pallid cheeks and gills;
Away they sped in haste, pell-mell,

To 'scape the monster, 'scaped from hell,—
    For that was what they thought,—
One chief alone, of all the rest,
Stood forth with brave, undaunted breast,
    And set its rage at naught.
Like sturdy oak he stood in path,
His flashing eyes and brows of wrath
    Fierce to intensity.
His stalwart form in awful pose
Above the wreck of ruin rose
    In swelling majesty.
As perfect as a stalk of wheat,
From skin of scalp to sole of feet
    He measured twelve feet three
    (The Cardiff giant sure was he).
Khalankhadula was his name,
Among his tribe, the first in fame,
    Born at Schenectady.
And there he stood with angry spear
    Poised o'er his feathered head,
Prepared to stop the wild career
    Of the terrific dread.
The monster eyed him, and with bound,
    Quick as the wink of Sphinx,
Was on him. Ere he turned around
His jellied body on the ground
    Was food for wolf and lynx.

On, on the monster flew and came
   Where Newburg, on the Hudson, stands;
And there its wearied limbs waxed lame,
   And Alliegundabago's hands.
Awhile, like a stupendous frog,
It mired in a moving bog,—
   Terrific were its squeals!
The chieftain, sliding from its back,
Climbed a great tree, to 'scape the pack
   Which followed at his heels.
And there he sat while frantic beast,
Predestined for a Wolf-lynx feast,
   Below him roared and raved,
And slashed with angered trunk and tail
The oozing bog, awhile the gale
   Its hungry nostrils craved,
Vibrated dolor, grunt, and moan,
Expiring sighs, and dying groan.
And while the wolves, convulsively,
Stripped flesh from bone with fiendish glee,
And lapped his gore deliriously,
As sinks in cloud the orb of day,
So sunk in ooze its form away;
And ere light faded into night,
With gurgling sound it passed from sight,—
   The last one of its race.
And there it was that years apast

Its frame was found in place,
Which, mounted well, and wired fast,
Gives Dr. Warren deathless fame,
And adds to Boston's mighty name.

EPISODE No. 2.

OFF CAPE COD.

Once on a time, when off Cape Cod,
  The chief in his dugout canoe,
Fishing for shark with line and rod,—
If 'twasn't so may heathen god
  Stripe Truth till black and blue!—
While seesawing, like gull at rest,
Upon old ocean's throbbing breast,
  Unruffled and serene,
Like thunderbolt from cloudless skies,
Charging his mind with wild surprise,
  Broke raging on the scene
A monster sword-fish, frenzy-eyed,
And horrid Octopus, beside,
  Engaged in hellish strife.
Around the excited waters boiled,
The seething foam with blood grew soiled,
  The struggle was for life,—
  The breezes died from fright;
While from each coral cleft and cave
Rose through the bright crest of each wave—
  Spectators of the fight—

Mermen and maids with faces dun,
   Green goggles o'er their eyes
   Of largest saucer size,
Which flashed like mirrors in the sun
   And dazzled in its light;
The chief upon the conflict gazed
Like one by fascination dazed,
   Awe-struck and fear-transfixed—
   His faculties all mixed—
Unable to escape; for, why?
His scull had 'scaped his hand and eye
   And floated out of reach,
   T'ward the pebbled beach;
Now on the surface, then in deep,
In narrowing circles did they sweep
   The crazy craft around;
An hundred feet in air they sprung
Then dropped the shiv'ring waves among
   And dived to depths profound,
   Where, with an insane bound,
They closed in conflict. Fierce they raged,
Sword, tail, and flipper, all engaged
   To conquer or to die;
And when again they reappeared
Through crimson waters, blubber-smeared,
   'Twas close by his canoe;
And for a moment there they lay,

Two monsters of the deep, at bay,
   Eying each other through,
Like Monitor and Merrimac,
Before they made that fierce attack
   Which satisfied each crew;
Spread out like Sinbad's isle the one,
The other like a great Krupp gun
   Nosed with gigantic sword.
Hate, like the flash from angry skies,
Shot from the storm-clouds of their eyes,
   And their wild passions gored.
Again they circled, when, from curl,
The waters hastened to a whirl
   Which, like Norse maelstrom, drew
Into its vortex boat and chief,
While loud he sang his song of grief,—
   "Oh, fleeting world, adieu!"
With sudden dive the monsters threw
Their dripping tails into the blue,
   And disappeared like flash,
The agile sword-fish in the lead,
The devil following him with speed
   Of meteor on a dash.
Down slid the chieftain in their wake,
Followed the great Sea Serpent snake
Which, like a log, had lain asleep
Upon the bosom of the deep,

Waves pillowing its head,
Until the echoes of the splash
'O'erwhelmed it like a thunder-crash
  And oped its eyes of lead;
Then piloted by trail of blood
Which crimsoned the devouring flood,
  It glided to the spot
  Where raged the battle hot;
And when it saw in the abyss
  Dugout and sachem spinning 'round,
And heard the surges' seething hiss
  Pregnate each air-wave with fierce sound,
A sudden fury stirred its strength
And shivered through its mighty length,
  Bristling each brazen scale.
Aloft it reared its horrid crest,
Curved loftily its vengeful breast,
  Glittering like burnished mail,
Then after, with a speed as swift
As lightning from the tempests rift,
  It flashed its rage to wreak.
While he, as calm as deviled saint,
Wiped with lace handkerchief the paint
  And brine from his ringed beak;
Then, as the horror slid apast
Like a weird phantom, grim and ghast,

Sent by the evil-eyed,
  He sped, like shaft, aside;
And, quick as thought, with spurt and gasp,
Seized its slimed tail with grim-death's grasp
  Of desperate desire,
And held till he was drawn away
From the intensity of day
Far down into the dim obscure,
Where in their dismal caves, secure,
  Coiled in their nested ire,
Repose the monsters of the deep,—
Leviathans whose slimy creep
  Disturbs the ocean's rest,
  And agitate its crest.
The water-dragons and the snakes,
Whose sinuous forms cleave burning lakes,
  Where hid volcanoes swell;
The dreadful salamander which
Feeds on the yellow flames of pitch,
  And guards the gates of hell.
The shark—dread terror of the wave—
  That gnaws the flesh from dead men's bones;
The vampire of the anguish cave,
  Where the damned spirit wails and moans;
All these he saw and dreadful forms
Begotten of the Fiend of Storms,—

Misshapen, vast, incarnate things,
    Which none but drowning men behold,—
With gorgon eyes, and fiery stings,
    Who guard the merchant's sunken gold,
And fierce on him they fixed their eyes,
Crazed with the terror of surprise.
And as he gazed his senses fled,
    Through his laxed grasp the serpent's tail
Slid like a streak. From out the dread,
    Like an embodied howling gale,
Toward him rushed with horrid spasm
    Of grinning mouth and frantic motion,
That hideous monster of the chasm,—
    The octopus of deepest ocean.
But ere its vampirish arms could coil
    About his languid frame,
And vise it in its cruel toil,
    Like a fierce myth of flame,
Flashed the great prehistoric whale,
    From dozing on the lee,
And with an angered stroke of tail
    Despatched it instantly,
    And paralyzed the sea.
Then from the insatiate maw of death,
    And its grim treachery,
It snatched the sachem, scant of breath,
    And, through the breakers sullen roar,

His limp, faint body safely bore,
And on Long Island's sea-girt shore
Unloaded him, at Montauk Point,
His nose and great toe out of joint.
And there with song and much ado,
The last Mohican brought him to.

EPISODE No. 3.

A DREAM HE DREAMED.

Returning once from hunting coon
And 'possum on the Callicoon,
　Along with blithe Colcrocket,
Their brains as full of sentiment
As ladies' 'kerchiefs full of scent,
　Or as a school-boy's pocket.
A sleep stole o'er them as they preyed
On oyster-bed in Belmont glade,—
　Off flew his mind like rocket!
And, as he dozed, appeared to him,
Perched in the crotch of shell-bark limb,
　A coon of glaring size.
A pipe of peace or piece of pipe,
Streaked 'round with thin vermilion stripe,
　Adorned his corn-juiced jaws
　And smoked his laughing eyes.
Embroidered moc'sins shod his feet,
A furry mantle clothed his meat.
　He paused to lick his paws
　And tail alive with play.

And there he sat in light of moon,
That independent same old coon,
   Whiling the time away.
His smoke-veiled countenance the while
O'ercast with frown or lit with smile,
   Until, like flash of day,
It vanished in the murky air,
Pursued by Nox's phantom mare,
   Which drew the sachem's mind away
Into a dismal, howling waste
Of shrieking ghosts by horrors chased
   Throughout the eternal day.
And one of them, a monster fright,
   With dragon-body brazen-scaled,
Great, icy, bat-like wings of night,
   And sea-horse rear all devil-tailed,
     Sped fiercely to his side;
Its bas'lisk eyes full of the fire
Of hate and desperate desire,
   Its red eyes open wide
As are the brassy gates of hell
When through their portals surge and swell
   Th' inebriate human tide.
Upon his cheeks he felt its breath,
Foul as the airs from caves of death.
   He strove in vain to hide
   Within the airy tide,

But on his front the monster placed
   Its leaden paws beset with claws,
And wound its tail around his waist.
   The while it snapped its fang-filled jaws,
And shot into his breast of sighs
The dreadful glitter of its eyes.
Moaning, he chilled, and shrieked aloud,
   As the fierce monster shook and spread
   Its fiery wings above its head,
And bore him in a flaming cloud
   To boundary of space,
From whence, with frantic squeak and squall,
It loosed its hold and let him fall,—
   Down, down, he fell, like shot,
   So swift he waved red hot.
The pygmies bridled up their geese,
   And followed him with speed.
The air-fiends strode each passing breeze,
   Each Fury gained its meteor-steed,
   And sought his glitt'ring track.
Vain the pursuit, for as he drew
Anear the earth Jove's eagle flew
   And beaked his breech-clouts slack,
And buoyed him safely to a spot
Beside a wild, sequestered grot,
   In an enchanted glade,

Where,
  Encircled by a haloed air,
A black-eyed, love-lorn maiden sat,
Upon a green Scotch-thistle mat,
  All Evishly arrayed,
Picking the music from the string
Of a celestial bobaling,
And sighing sea-shellodiously,—
"Oh, would my true love were with me;
  With love his soul I'd fire,
Until, in blissful raptures, he
  Would gloriously expire."

As peeping Tom, of Coventry,
  Sought with rude eyes to drink
A priceless draught of chastity
  Athrough the lattice chink,
The sachem, through the quiv'ring leaves,
Where roved the flowers' perfume thieves,
  Sweet spirits of the breeze,
Peered with a mind-absorbing look,
Like youth through a forbidden book
  Of wanton mysteries,
And strove to catch in toil of sighs
The vagrant glances of her eyes,
  Which danced the shadows through.

But peered he vainly till a breeze,
In ecstasy of ecstasies,
And drunken with the balmed perfume
Of spice and pine and honeyed bloom,
In loving pity swayed the trees
Into aerial harmonies,
  And gave her to his view.
Instant from his dazed sight he sent
A ravished glance incontinent
  Upon her faultless form.
As glorious seemed she to his sight
As when the moon of Summer night
  Peeps through the scud of storm.
He gazed enraptured. Through his frame
Shot passions sublimated flame,
  Which set his brains aglow.
Impetuously he sought the spot
Where sat the maiden of the grot,
  When at him hawked a raven,
    The guardian of the spot,
    With seething anger hot;
  Its frantic caws and bloody beak,
  Its cruel claws and quaking squeak,
    Its glossy ruffled plumes
    Of deepest midnight glooms,
  Turned him, a moment, craven.

Up sprung the maiden, and away
  In agony of dread,
Like sunbeam through the rainbowed spray,
  With glowing feet she sped
Into the silence of the night,
  By haunted forests dim,
Where mortals shudder with affright,
  And weird Chimeras hymn
Their mournful pæans to the breeze,
Which thrills with fear the sleeping trees.

The chief, like stag pursuing doe,
With frantic bound and heart aglow,
  Followed her shining trail
O'er hill and mount and stream and plain,
Through Fantasy's ghost-filled domain
  And each enchanted vale.
Pursuit beamed from his eager eye:
Possession! was his spirit's cry.
  On, on, he flew, until
The maiden down Niagara's stream
Whirled in canoe of watery beam,
  Like coaster down a hill,
While he, astride a vagrant log,
Through the cool atmosphere of fog,
  Pushed from the rocky shore.

Flew the white foam-flakes creamily,
Danced the illusions dreamily,
  Before his moon-beam oar.
The titt'ring stars and smiling moon
  Gazed on them as they sped,
While from mid-air a phantom coon,
  With eyeballs crimson red,
Cried, "Alliegundabago, oar!
Chaunt Io! Ho! Excelsior!
Hoop-la! My duck on stilts, wade in!
None but the brave deserve to win!"
Away, away, log and canoe
Danced feathery o'er the waters blue,
  As if imbued with life.
Like streamer of the Northern light
The maiden's hair flashed through the night;
  Her eyes those of mad wife:
Swelled mournfully along the shore
The rushing current's hollow roar,
  The hoot-owl's dismal cry,
While panther's shriek and eagle's scream
Broke from the forests of his dream,
  And Echo made reply.

The rapids seized and bore them past,
Like rusted leaves by breath of blast,
  Toward the enchanted falls,

Whose thunder filled the air with sound,
Which shuddered through the dim profound,
   And died by heaven's walls.
On, on, a single length ahead
The sachem's log, the maiden sped.
   The prize was almost won,
When o'er the falls into the blue
Expanse of moonlit spray she flew,
   Her countenance like sun,
Toward him turned; awhile her thumb,
With scornful fingers frolicksome
   Wagged from her sneering nose;
And as the panting chief, red hot,
Adown the falling waters shot,
   In admirable pose,
Dissolved she like a meteor's blaze,
Into the azure of the haze;
   And, like the viewless wind,
   Left not a trace behind.
"Maid of the mist, I've missed you!" he
Shrieked, in delirious agony;
   The wind caught up the cry,
And on the fragrance of the day,
With coyish echo stole away,
   And hid in depth of sky;
And when into the seething deep,
Wave-shot he plunged with breathless sweep,

And gasp and throe and choke,
Scream after scream disturbed his rest,—
Colcrocket struck him on the breast,—
And, trembling, he awoke.

SUICIDE.—A VISION.

Tired of the world's corroding cares,
Its pleasures and deluding snares,
I sought my couch. 'Twas midnight, and
The storm-king reigned o'er sea and land,
Quaking the earth with thunders dire,
Emblazoning the air with fire,
And torturing to deeds of death
Old ocean with his cycloned breath.
I sought my couch my mind oppressed
With fancies which my soul depressed,
And which, like furies, racked my brain
Until my spirit writhed in pain
And drove my vagrant thoughts insane.
I wished to dream, and, dreaming, yield
My spirit to the unrevealed,
And in the silent halls of sleep
Forever dwell in slumbers deep.
While thus revolving in my mind
The means t' attain the end designed,
Uprose, I thought, from out the sea
Of troubles which environed me
A monster, fearful in its mien,
Which waking eye had never seen!

Its varying form of flesh seemed scaled
With adamant, which triple-mailed
Its vulnerable parts. Its wings
  Were dragon-like, of sheeted flame;
Its tail, like serpents', barbed with stings;
  Hued was it as the blush of shame;
Charged was its breast with frantic ire;
Its eyes seemed orbs of living fire;
Its nostrils shed contagion, while
  The vapors of its sulph'rous breath
Reeked pestilent, envenomed guile
  Fraught with the subtleness of death.
Stained were its fangs with human gore
Which from its mouths in streams a score
Spurted. 'Twas horrible to see!
Unmanned, I shrieked, "Ah, woe is me!"
        With trembling dread
I quaked, and turned away my head,
While through my frame a terror stole
Whose icy touch congealed my soul.
"O God!" I cried, "extend thine aid
And guide me to some Cretan shade
Where I may bide till darkest night
Cancels the vision to my sight."
Then through an atmosphere of flame
Towards my couch the monster came:

"I am the gracious world!" it roared;
"Of earth, and all therein, the lord,—
The power that, with vengeful hate,
Will haunt thee to perdition's gate,—
Behold, and tremble!" Fiery look!
I shrunk in dread, my couch forsook,
And strove to hide in secret nook.
In vain. The monster's searching glance
Sought for and found my countenance,
And charged my anguished mind with dread.
Into the night my fancies fled,
And through the air of witchery,
Haunted by shapes of sorcery,
My ghostly terrors followed me,
Till on the verge of blank despair
I stood in abject fear and prayer.
Swooning I fell. 'Twas then I heard
A babelade of sounds absurd,
Like choristry of unclean bird,
And saw flash through the murky gloom
The childhood spectres of the tomb;
While in that atmosphere of flame
Fiends hovered round and hissed my name;
Each searching glance the while divined
The guilty secrets of my mind,
Diffusing through my frame a chill
Which deadened sense and conquered will.

"Here are the means, misfortune's heir,
To 'scape the grim world's tort'ring care,"
They then exclaimed sarcastically,
Exhibiting their deviltry,
While fire-haired one with flaming crest
   Shot from his glittering eyes of hate
A subtle frenzy through my breast,
   The mock of life the doom of fate.
Then one with harpy's front and wing
Flew at me like a stone from sling,
And, chatt'ring, grinned derisively;
Awhile its talons offered me
A glittering razor, whose blue blade
Was with the gore of crime inlaid.
Swifter than light, with sin'ster gloat,
Flashed the keen steel across its throat,
Then faded from my mind; awhile
A harpy, with sardonic smile,
Offered a cord, and eyed a beam
Which shadowed a tumultuous stream;
Then craned its neck and lolled its tongue,
And rolled its eyes as if 'twere hung,
As, fluttering, it gazed aslant
On flood with looks significant.
A third one, as it flickered up,
Poured viewless drops in airy cup,

And, feigning sleep, with mimic cough,
Assumed, with smirk, to toss it off;
Then writhed its face, its foul wings crossed,
And blanched like flow'r when nipped by frost.
A fourth disguised as imp of fun,
With ghastly phiz and ghostly plumes,
Emerged from charcoal's deadly fumes,
Snatched from the misty air a gun,
Its muzzle placed its brow anear,
Claw-pulled its trigger; while, with sneer,
A scarlet demon offered me,
With hell-engendered mimicry,
A cocked revolver, while it spread
Its vaporous wings above its head.
I shuddered as I felt my soul
Pass from my flesh through bullet-hole.
And heard it curse with oath its birth
As echoingly it sped from earth.
Frosted with horror, sore dismayed,
Seized I a razor, tried its blade,
But hurled it from me as a chill
Suffused my frame and froze my will.
Then did I cast my gaze on high,
Caught swaying cord, but with deep sigh
Dropped it, and shrunk from stream so nigh;
Clutched poisoned chalice, and essayed
To drink the contents while I prayed.

But ere my palate tasted, came
From out the night a voice of blame,
Which cried,—

   "Thou fool! how very wise,
Thou turn'st to Hell not Paradise.
How vain! eluding human ill
By bartering soul and strangling will!
Coward! afraid of myths that flee
If you but meet them manfully!
Dolt! hurling the immortal where
Fiends gnash their teeth 'mid dull despair."
Before it ceased, in chorus broke,
Like screams through suffocating smoke,
The voices of a spectral crew,—
Though never one addressed my view,—
"Fool! to believe what thou dost hear,"
   They groaned;
   Then moaned,—
"Let it in this and out that ear;"
   And sighed,—
"Your form is naught but fashioned clay,
Which, soulless, gusts will puff away;"
   Then cried,—
"You're but a grain in harvest, or
A mote of sand on ocean's shore;
A drop within Time's shoreless sea;
An atom of infinity."

Awhile, extemporaneously,
A gibbering myth of sound essayed
To edify, and, ass-like, brayed,—
"Your soul is but a vital spark
One moment bright, the next all dark,
And as the wave of life retires,
It flickers, struggles, and expires."

"There is no God!" a deep voice gleeked;
"Nor heaven nor hell!" a thin one squeaked;
"No resurrection, no hereafter,"
A third voice whined with childish laughter,
While imp of thought, bepuffed with pride,
Chuckled,—"Death comes, our spirits glide
To new-born swine,—and there abide,—
From which, through nature, soon evolved,
We pass to donkeys,—brute resolved,—
And so progress till time-dissolved."
"Life's but a dream—a wakeful trance;
We're but the slaves of circumstance;
All things do come and go by chance,"
Insidiously chimed voices three,
In measured strains, sepulchrally,
As twitt'ring myth with feeble lisper
To my rapt sense essayed to whisper,—
"Deluded man! of dust the brother!
This earth's your hell, there is none other."

As fancy's tuneful argosy
Glides o'er the waves of Fantasy
Until engulfed in harmony,
So sailed each dreamy voice away
Into the shadow of the day,
And through a labyrinth of sound
Vibrated to the weird profound
Until in depth of distance drowned.

I wooed belief, but clouds of doubt
Encompassed my dazed mind about,
Till reason, for a time, gained sway,
And bade me hurl the cup away,
Dissolving every doubt, as light
Dissolves the shadows of the night.
Then before my vision rose,
Like spectral wraiths from moonlit snows,
An apparition saintly-fair,
All habited in samite rare,
  With glowing, beatific face
And speaking eyes and radiant hair,
  And visionary form of grace,
Which, like a cloud, enveloped me
In odorous mists of sanctity.
Spell-bound, my every sense absorbed,
And in her blessed presence orbed,

I stood. 'Twas then a thought revealed
Her as my guardian, strength, and shield,
The being who from infancy
Until I gained maturity
Through dangers seen and unseen had
  My vagrant footsteps led,
Had balmed my woes, my heart made glad,
  And soothed my anguished head.
Then rippled on my dreamy ear
Her spirit-voice, celestial clear,—
"Beloved one, beware! beware
The Tempter's wiles, the Demon's snare!
Oh, shun them! else in torments dire
Thy soul, a vital shade of fire
Fraught with ungratified desire,
Through space will float and ne'er expire.
Heed not the voices! they delude
Your hungry mind with devil's food,
And with a Judas-kiss betray
Your consecrated life away;
Still hold the faith which infancy
Learned at thy sainted mother's knee:
The earth-born lore of fools despise
And rest thy hopes on Paradise."

'Twas then her eyes, with sorrow laden,
Upon me cast a fond adieu,

While she evanished in the blue
Which veils the stars and curtains Aidenn.
Transfixed I stood, amazed and dazed,
And where her finger pointed gazed.

Uprose, like a gigantic tower,
An arm of superhuman power,
Which grew each moment, till its hand
Shone like a meteor o'er the land,
And the cerulean of the skies
Parted, till my illumined eyes
Discerned the hills of Paradise.

Then through the soft effulgence shone
The rays which beam from Glory's throne,
And in their lucid splendors I
A lustrous cross could well descry
Superlatively clear and bright;
Yet, to my soul's enraptured sight,
As gentle as the beams of night,
A subtle radiance girt it round;
With hallowed glory was it crowned,
While flowers of life about it wound.
Upon it hung, in human guise,
The incarnate Sovereign of the skies,

Just as He hung on Calvary's height,
  Save that His body purified
Of earthly dross shone heavenly-white,
  And, sunlike, shed a wondrous tide
Of living glory which all space
And systems of the universe
Pervaded. Every living thing
Of locomotion, scale, or wing
Breathed of its ether, while the trees,
Rocks, earth, and waters, and the breeze
Absorbed its radiance, and athrough
Its attributes lived, changed, and grew.

Beneath the cross a lustrous book
Caught my rapt sight and bade me look
Upon its page inspired, and
Directed me to that command
Expressive of the Sovereign will,—
Which there I read, "*Thou shalt not kill!*"
Like sorrow, through my 'wildered brain
There flashed an agony of pain,
And, like a baleful star, quick sped
Throughout my mind an awful dread.
I felt like guilty wretch, and stood
Like blasted tree in storm-wrecked wood,
Lifeless, without a hope to hold
My spirit in its loving fold.

Then from the cross a gentle voice
　　Sweet as angelic symphony
Inspired me with a sweet rejoice
　　And warmed me with humanity;
It bade me fix my doubt-tossed mind
On Him, the Saviour of mankind,
And fly the crafty demon's wiles,
His glozing words and artful smiles,
　　　　Saying,—
"Weak creature of my sovereignty,
Like simple child rely on me
And do my will! and when, in time,
Thy spirit seeks the realm sublime,
Exalted thou shalt rule, and be
Blest through a vast eternity."

'Twas then it seemed that, like a ray
Of moonlight 'neath the sun's first sway,
The cross dissolved in radiant spray;
And then, supernal, in its stead,
Through the ethereal's crimson red,
Appeared a throne miraculous,
Electrically luminous,
As boundless as the universe,
Far-reaching as the primal curse,
Sublime as the deep seas of space,
Majestic as the hills of grace,

And on it beamed the Crucified
Of Calvary's mount, beatified,
Illimitably magnified,—
Himself again. Absorbing sight!
O form of uncreated light!
O awful vision of the night!
O being of supreme delight!
O mystery of mysteries!
O star-crowned god of deities!
O holy fount of love divine!
O life of consecrated wine!
O majesty of noonday's sun!
The Lord of lords! the Three in One!
The living Word! the Truth! the Light
Of grovelling superstition's night!
The omnipotent Redeemer! The
Life! The incarnate Mystery!
The Judge immaculate! He, who
Unfolded heaven to human view!
The Holy One! Immanuel!
Death's conqueror, and scourge of hell!
The grand Incomprehensible!
The Being incorruptible!
The great wide, deep, unfathomable!
The Eternal One! The Law of Laws!
The All-in-All! The primal Cause.

Enchanted, awed, and ravished quite,
Blinded through fierce excess of light,
In joyousness my senses passed,
In trance before that vision vast.

Then, while my soul its vigil kept,
Aerially before me swept,
Like sunbeams through the atmosphere
Which girdles this terrestrial sphere,
A multitude of bright souls shaped
To spirits, gloriously draped
In limpid splendors, every one
In the full tide of Glory's sun,
Which, in its far-off majesty,
Shed its benignant beams on me,
And charged my soul with ecstasy.
There, too, a host of glittering forms
 On missions from the court divine
Unto the worlds, like flash of storms,
 Shot dazzling through the starry shine,
While from the spheres came thronging hosts
Of spectral, disembodied ghosts;
And with them, by fair angels led,
The bright Intelligences sped,
And round their holy influence shed.

Floating amid the calm between
My soul and that great throne serene,

Arrayed in limpidness of sheen,
A choir of seraphs caught my gaze,
Enrapturing heav'n with anthemed praise,
Star-censers swaying, while the air,
Pregnant with incensed love and prayer,
Bore to the Father's gracious ears
The worship of revolving spheres.
Beyond, through mists of dazzling sheen,
By mortal vision never seen,
Moved myriad forms of Seraphim,
Before whose brightness stars waned dim,
All warbling to th' Æolian strains
Of winds which sighed o'er heavenly plains,
And to the organed harmonies
Of stars and universal seas.

There, too, celestially fair,
The cherubs of the upper air
In shining troops appeared awhile.
In shining crowns with radiant smile,
And, floating where Archangels soar
Adoring, round th' exalted choir
  Of dazzling Cherubim,
Mingled their dulcet harmonies
Of rapt cherubic ecstasies
  With glorifying hymn.

Then 'mid the star-mist gloriously
   Appeared, sun-robed, the saints of yore,
And by them shone illustriously
   The martyrs whom the Christ-world bore,
Each shining like a beam of light,
Yet, in degree, as stars of night,
Accordingly as each had kept
The faith for which his life he left.
Kings did they seem, and emperors,
   For all their brows were nimbus crowned,
These who had gained th' Elysian shores,
   And heard the echoes of its sound,
Permitted there to feast their sight
With glory from the Fount of Light,
And taste the untold joys of those
Who'd gained through death their soul's repose.

Then did my soul relapse from trance
   To swoon, and then to dream, and then
A mocking myth, with subtlest lance,
   Shot swift as flash upon my ken,
And with a fierce, malignant thrust,
   It sped with fury through my brain,
And clogged its cells with hellish lust,
   And tortured it with thoughts insane.

I felt like one adrift on sea
   Of sublimated misery;

Without a hope to cheer the gloom
Which haunted it like fiend of doom,
Augmenting, with its sullenness,
The agony of my distress.

A friendless waif, I seemed by all
Deserted. Life was bitterest gall;
A burden, heavy to be borne;
And I, a wretch, a thing of scorn,
Beyond redemption's glorious scheme,
Beyond salvation's searching beam,
With naught to yield me peace, or calm
My soul with consolation's balm,—
What cared I for? The voices lied
Unto my mind unsanctified!
The visions came from thoughts profane;
But phantasies of tortured brain;
And the dread teachings of the Word
Were idle vagaries. Absurd
Old Women fables, sanctified
By antique time, and deified
By priestly dreamers to excite
The stupid world to fear and fright;
To threat, cajole, and terrify;
True or untrue, I fain would die:
Hell, heaven, or naught! 'twas all the same.
Eternal bliss, change, trance, or flame,

What mattered it? 'Twas destiny:
At most but change of misery;
'Twas *Kismet*, fate,—as 'twas to be.

Just then the monster's sullen roar
Assailed my ears and vexed me sore,
Until, on desperation's brink
I stood, and ceased to muse or think;
Awhile into the depths undreamed
I peered. Then seemed that from it streamed
A voice aerial, sweet as sleep,
Which sighed,—
    "Why hesitate to leap?
Behind, the world and wretchedness;
Before, a heaven of happiness;
Come, wretch, and in the unknown find
Freedom from pain, relief for mind,—
A land of bliss and golden hours,
Of endless joys and fadeless flowers.
Why linger, mortal? Why delay?
Come to our radiant land, away!"

Then hov'ring o'er oblivion's brink,
Into whose waves I fain would sink,
Fell that winged voice whose eloquence
Of guiling music wooed me hence.

SUICIDE.—A VISION.

As falls on ears of mariner
   The siren's 'wildering melody,
So fell on mine, celestial clear,
   Her spirit-soothing symphony:
"Come, wretched mortal," thus she sighed,
   "Come to our joyous state and be
Free from th' incarnate evil-eyed,
   Blest through a vast eternity."

Bewildered, fascinated, dazed,
My mind by cruel mem'ries crazed,
Unconsciously I stood and gazed,
Until a power beyond resist,
Evoked from out the ghostly mist,
Impelled me.
          From the awful height
I plunged into the gloom of night;
And as I sped, broke on my ear
A scornful laugh so shrill and clear
It thrilled the swooning atmosphere
And filled my soul with frantic fear.
Awhile I saw the tempter turned
Into a ghoul, whose eyeballs burned
With hate's red fire, which seemed to roll
Malignant fury through my soul;
Like shaft of light from Dian's bow
Athrough the darkness did I go

So swift that my illumined hair,
Torn from the scalp by rushing air,
Was caught by howling gusts, and whirled,
Like threads of fire, on the world.
Then through my mind with magic speed
Flashed all my life,—each thought, word, deed,
All I had done from hour of birth
Until I spurned the doleful earth.
I realized my wickedness,
And scorched with agonized distress.

On, on, I flew. My stifled breath
Fled from my frame. I lived in death;
And as my body grew to dust
And mingled with each passing gust,
My shadowy immortality
Flashed starlike through immensity.

I lived—O God! and through the blaze
Which tinged the gloom with purple haze
Saw starting from the dread abyss
Where hell's red waters seethe and hiss
Squadrons of fiends on flaming wings
And talons all alive with stings,
Who flashed apast me like the glint
Of angry spears, their eyes of flint

Upbraiding me with dev'lish squint
Awhile they mocked with gibe and jeer.
"Ha! ha!" they laughed, "the tempter lied:
Hell is thy doom, damned suicide!"
On with the speed of thought I sped
Through the dim region of the dead,
Whose ghastly shadows filled my sight
With frightful visions of the night,
And with a grief devoid of tears
Blasted my soul with frantic fears.
Then burst to flame the stifling air
With intense lightning's blinding glare,
And round th' shudd'ring worlds of space
   Ten million angry thunders dashed
Like vengeful angels shorn of grace,
   And 'gainst the gates of heaven crashed.
Blinded with glare and stunned by sound,
A shadowy form I whirled around
The blank void of the dim profound,
Till, quickened into sense, I heard
A sound like seas when tempest-stirred,
And then a trumpet's blast so clear
That from it shrunk the atmosphere,
And like a parchment sheet, hand-rolled,
The blazing firmament was scrolled,
And, quick as thought, I stood alone
Before th' Eternal's dazzling throne.

Oh, anguish inexpressible!
Oh, agony no tongue can tell!
As from the living glory came
With withering voice my mortal name
And then my sentence: "Suicide!
  Thou who with knowledge scorned my will,
  My laws defied with guilty skill;
  Now from mine angered presence go,
And with the damned fore'er abide
  Accursed in deepest depth of woe."

In twinkle of a vagrant ray
Through gaseous void I sped away
On breath of flame which seemed to me
To throb and pulse like troubled sea.
O Christ! the torment! the despair!
Mind cannot think nor pen declare!
I breathed the air of blasphemy;
Absorbed the subtle deviltry;
And, flaming, gasped deliriously.
Each idle word and thought profane,
Each blighting curse and deed inane,—
The offsprings of my mortal brain,—
Vibrating through immensity,
In spirit-guise returned to me,
And with a frantic, wild endeavor
To rend my soul, assailed me ever,

Upbraiding with their blasphemies
Me for their doleful miseries.

So, too, I saw and comprehended
   The dire effect of word and act,
As with my faculties they blended
   And ceaselessly my conscience racked;
And saw, and fully comprehended,
   What would have been if word and act
Accorded with what God intended
   When souls were made a human fact.

Then each vile act of life in guise
Of Fury's shape flashed on my eyes,
Inquisitors' vindictive glee
Fresh tortures adding constantly,
While ever growing came to me
My sins in their enormity.
Around I heard but could not see
   The agonizing heaven-cursed souls
Of those who'd spurned the world like me,
   And saw flit by in guise of ghouls
The terrors of eternity;
And as my sleepless conscience fired
   The anguish of my spirit-mind,
My voice, with agony inspired,
   Swelled with the rest to warn mankind.

Then through me shot, like storm-cloud's flash,
  A thrill of terror,—with the stroke!
As on my ear fell with the crash:
  All shuddering, screaming, I awoke.

•

THE END.

www.ingramcontent.com/pod-product-compliance
Lightning Source LLC
Chambersburg PA
CBHW022112160426
43197CB00009B/989